BUILD A BUSINESS

DISCOVER THE TRUE EARNING POTENTIAL OF SELF EMPLOYMENT BY BUILDING A BUSINESS THE PROFITABLE WAY

** Two Books in One – "Start Your Own Business" and "Be a Boss" **

By K. Connors

TABLE OF CONTENTS

START YOUR

OWN BUSINESS

LEARN HOW SUCCESSFUL ENTREPRENEURS CAN TURN ANY IDEA INTO A PROFIT

By K. Connors

INTRODUCTION

Whether you're struggling to find employment or simply wanting to be your own boss, looking to start your own business is exactly the right thing to do for many people. However, I'm not here to sugar coat it for you. On the road to success lies many shattered dreams and tattered ambition. This information will help you give yourself the best chance of success. Ahead of anything else is making that first move. Though starting your own business is never an easy challenge, it is important to be aware that the perfect moment is never likely to come. There is no time like the present. Possessing the focus and the ability to shrug off lingering worries and press ahead is often the key to success.

Having a particular market to explore, perhaps a niche area not presently filled will help. If so, the earlier you start the better things will most likely be. Being aware of the local climate is essential since even seemingly inaccessible industries will present excellent opportunities. Of course, coming up with a unique idea or breaking into a new market can be incredibly difficult - and is where many new businesses fail.

Sometimes though, as the old adage goes, you fail to see the wood for the trees, so considering things that may be staring you right in the face is important. Look at whether there are any professional services that local businesses are not being provided with. If provided for, are the current services really up to the task? Perhaps start your own business on that basis.

If in employment already, consider if there are any suppliers that management is consistently complaining about. Ask yourself if you could do better. Many individuals attain personal success by first identifying a problem, and then working to solve it.

With a plan in place, knowing whether you already possess the necessary skills, or have yet to attain them, is important. You most likely already have one of the most important skills - the drive to start your own business. If you do not have the actual skills to deliver the product, then working out a way to attain them is the next step.

Consider whether there is a franchisor offering a franchise opportunity in the business sector you are interested in.

Respected franchises are clearly doing something right, have excellent training in place, business knowledge, and a proven model to give you the great start that can feel impossible with brand new enterprises. Most importantly though, a good franchisor provides expertise and essential support. In essence, it is your own business with the support of a successful chain. From helping to locate a viable area in which to start a business, to assisting with the logistics of setting up the premises, there is much to be gained from being part of a franchise.

Every business needs funding, and getting this in place is often the toughest challenge. Not securing the financing can end many of the best-planned ambitions, though lenders are eager to invest in strong opportunities. Again, franchisees with a proven business model can help secure funding far easier than start-ups, making it an increasingly viable option if you want to start your own business.

REASONS TO START YOUR OWN BUSINESS

People all over the world are searching for new ways to make money. However, they are somewhat confused on the direction they should take. In addition, some people are confused as to why people are going the "entrepreneurial" route instead of the educational route. In my opinion, I believe that someone should exercise all opportunities to make money. Whether it is going to school or starting your own business, I believe that this world is too insecure to have only one source of income.

Below are reasons why some people are looking into starting their own businesses.

1. Make your own hours

2. You get to call the shots

3. You can create your work environment

4. You can pursue your own passion

5. You get to create your own ideas from scratch

Although people are looking into starting their own business, home businesses are on the rise because of the convenience to the owner. Not to mention some of the tax benefits as well... People love the ability to discipline themselves and work in their pajamas. In the real world, most employees are at the mercy of the companies who employ them. If your child is sick, in most cases, you must still go to work. In the workforce, you are only allowed a certain amount of days you are able to call off.

Here Are Some More Reasons

6. You are able to meet new people

7. You get to build your own team

8. You get to help people

9. You are able to invest in yourself

10. Earning potential is much higher

11. You become financially independent

12. You get tax benefits

13. You get to connect with your customers

14. You get to avoid boring tasks

15. You get to discover new fields

16. You get to become a mentor and inspire others

Is it possible for you to earn a living through owning your own business? 6 out of 10 businesses fail within the first year due to lack of education. Luckily for you, there are successful companies that offer free advice on the proper steps to take to create a lucrative business.

Although there are many resources available on the internet, the most important thing for you to note is, you must take the time to figure out what industry you would like to be involved in and what are your strengths as a person. If you are able to figure out who you are as a person, you will be able to find the perfect niche to be involved in.

CHAPTER ONE

JUST DO IT

For those who dream of having your own business, you're not alone. It's estimated that about 600,000 new businesses are started every year. In the event you're one of the many thousands of individuals trying to determine how to start your own business, this is a great place to begin. Starting your own business offers many benefits - more freedom, the potential to earn more, significant tax advantages, the opportunity to arrange your work life in a manner that works best for you, the possibility of building a beneficial asset you'll be able to sell or give away to your children. The list goes on and on.

Of course, there are challenges and risks, as well. But with some good planning and just a little education, you'll be able to reduce these dramatically. In truth, there has never been a greater time in history to start your own business. The Internet and everything it offers - just about limitless access to information, the power to simply and quickly talk with others, prompt access to specialists in every field, the chance to leverage your effort and time - make exploring how to start your own business easier and more efficient than ever.

Many people make the mistake of leaping into some sort of business without closely considering what they're doing and how to best do it. That's where sites like this can help. There are so many different types of companies out there right now - on-line businesses like Web marketing, on-line retailing, etc.; networking, advertising, franchises, etc. Making an attempt to resolve what to pursue might be overwhelming, especially because so many companies are hyped up with advertising and promotions.

The best advice is to do your homework, read books and others like it. Examine various kinds of businesses. Read opinions from those who are already doing it. Find packages that offer step-by-step instruction or training. Take some time to do it right, and you will be a lot happier and successful in the long run.

There are plenty of resources on-line - useful websites, informative articles, tons of ideas and advice.

All right there at your disposal, whenever you want them. Home businesses have been becoming more and more important throughout years. If the events of the past few years have taught us nothing else, they have proven that there isn't as much job security out there anymore as we would hope. The only security, the only guaranteed future, is the one you create for yourself.

Don't let another year pass with anything to show but an unfulfilled dream. Get started learning how to start your own business at this time! There is no cause to delay. There is an abundance of information accessible all over the place; anyone can do it!

Bear in mind, there's no time like the present! And no better future than the one you create for yourself. Start educating yourself on how to start your own business today! Just do it.

THE FIRST STEP IN STARTING YOUR OWN BUSINESS

The first step in starting your own business is to perform a thorough research on the kind of business to set up. It is through research that you will be able to identify the business opportunities you can engage in. After you have found out the various areas you can engage in you will be able to choose the area that suits you best. The main reason why many businesses fail shortly after commencing is because of a failure to perform a serious research on a business idea before implementing it.

By researching you are able to understand consumer needs, tastes and preferences. By doing so you will be able to provide what the consumers require. This would mean more sales resulting in high profits which are the objective of almost all businesses. The other reason why research is the first step in starting your own business is that through research, one is able to see both the pros and cons of entering certain niche markets.

The best location of your business is another important factor one will learn after conducting research. It is also very important for one to research before commencing a business in order to find the appropriate distribution channels. This is because you may have the right product and charge the right prices, but it may fail to reach the intended audience.

For your business to perform well it must be properly promoted. The correct advertising technique must be adopted in order to reach the targeted group. For all of the above to be achieved, the correct choice of promotion must be made. It is almost impossible to get the choice right without performing research, and that is why it is the first step in starting your own business. There are certain types of businesses that are very heavily taxed and charged by the government. In order to avoid such mistakes, the proper research must be conducted on various government policies and regulations before setting up the business.

Moreover, before beginning a business of your own, you must clearly understand all that it entails before you jump right in; the kind of licenses or permits you will need to obtain and the kind of products or services that are illegal and as such should be avoided. You will only learn this when you conduct your research. It is, therefore, necessary that you undertake this research as the first step in starting your own business.

CHAPTER TWO

DO I BUILD FROM SCRATCH OR BUY A FRANCHISE?

There are literally millions of people who attempt to start up some form of business each year around the globe. From those millions, hundreds of thousands succeed in starting it, and a far fewer number succeed in maintaining that business. For most, they are deterred and are ultimately unsuccessful. For others, their businesses do start up, but plummet within the first year. The lucky few who make it owe their success to an unlimited number of factors. For the potential business owners of the world, one way to improve your chances of success is to buy pre-owned. Instead of starting up your own business from scratch, buying an existing business or business idea can really help you be successful. There are many benefits in buying and taking over an existing business.

One of the largest deterrents of a new business is the idea of building it from scratch. You have to mold and perfect your business idea and formulate plans, work to gather a niche, attack the market, compete and stand out and ultimately cross your fingers and hope for the best; whereas, with a pre-existing business, most of that groundwork is already covered and perfected.

You can purchase a pre-existing business in a number of different ways. Maybe you have your eye on a restaurant or bar that is going out of business and you think you have the right recipe to get it back on its feet. Perhaps the owner of a business is retiring and wants to sell off his or her business. Or, you can purchase a franchise and take over the responsibility that way.

Regardless of how you acquire an existing business, the advantages are evident. For starters, the business is ready for immediate operations. Someone else has already gotten the business up and running. This also means that you should experience some quick cash flow, especially from existing inventory and/or clients. You can possibly generate income from the first day. Your customer base is also solidified. Instead of seeking out a new market, you can simply work to broaden your existing one. Since the business has a track record, the finances will be easier to maintain.

When it comes to competition, you can buy your way into a business that already has the market cornered. Some disadvantages exist, as well, so it's not all wine and roses here.

The cost of purchasing an existing business can sometimes be higher since you're paying for an operating business. The owner could have kept some serious problems hidden from you in order to sell off quickly. If you're a strong-willed person, you may meet some resistance from existing personnel within the business.

You could be dealing with obsolete goods. Apart from the higher costs, however, a bit of research into the business you wish to buy can reveal the rest of these flaws. With a little bit of work, you can correct any problems before you settle into your new business.

THINGS TO KNOW ABOUT FRANCHISING AND FRANCHISE OPPORTUNITIES

Franchising is proving to be the most resilient and effective way to undertake large-scale expansions. Many corporations, particularly those based in the U.S., have undertaken significant expansion and to some extent diversification through this route. The fact that both the franchiser and franchisee have a stake in the success of the store or the outlet coupled with the fact that the appointed franchisees are usually indigenous people with good understanding of local laws, it already has the interest of all parties involved; this coupled with the international and modern best practices of the franchise enables scope for considerable synergy.

Franchise cost: Franchise cost generally depends on the following factors,

1.   FRANCHISE FEE:

It is necessary to understand all services that are included in this fee because some franchises include land survey, expertise and skill development cost, and their trademark and logo cost, whereas some charge the franchise fee as a cost for just using the trademark and logo.

2.   LEGAL FEES:

Since the transactions are fairly large, you may have to consult your legal team to advise you about UFOC (Uniform Franchise Offering Circular). It is important to understand that since every franchise outlet is different and hence there may be a variation in costs.

3.   WORKING CAPITAL:

 As with any business it is important to keep your business well capitalized for day to day transactions.

4. INITIAL SETUP COSTS INCLUDING INVENTORY AND SUPPLIES NEEDS TO BE CONSIDERED

Franchise Opportunities: As with any other business there are a lot of franchise opportunities depending on your budget. There are franchise opportunities which cater to a wide range of budget estimates and also cut across various sectors, so there needs to be a balance between what you like or desire and what you can afford.

WHY GO FOR FRANCHISING?

If you are tired of your corporate job, and if you no longer wish to operate under someone else, you can either run a start-up of your own, or you can purchase a franchise. If you decide to run your own startup, you have to consider the risks involved. Firstly, you will be starting from scratch. So, you will have to build your brand name from the bottom up. You have to build a customer base from scratch as well, as you will be a new business on the market. In addition, you will have to break even with the high costs involved in running a start up.

If the risks involved in a start up leave you disgruntled, you may consider buying a franchise instead. When you buy a franchise, you are actually buying the business model of an existing company to serve a specific locality. For instance, if you know of a successful fast food chain that is open to franchising, you can buy the franchise and sell their goods under their banner and retain the majority of the profits. You function exactly as the parent company functions.

The main advantage with franchising is that you do not have to shoulder as many risks. Usually, the parent company is a well-known company. So, the brand name is already established. The brand is likely to have a loyal customer base in the area you plan to serve as well. The market is already there, you only have to service it. Where there is an existing market for your services, there you will also find profit to be made.

Secondly, the training for the staff is provided by the franchise at a fixed cost, in addition to the initial price of the franchise. You do not have to conduct any training. All you have to do is focus on running the business successfully.

Even though you have bought the business model of a company, you are not completely answerable for your work. As long as you maintain the brand image of the company, you are only answerable to yourself with regards to your hard work and discipline.

If you are interested in franchising, there are many businesses for sale that you can look into. Franchise opportunities are increasing as more and more companies and individuals are realizing the profitability of the venture in the long run.

ADVANTAGES OF BUYING A FRANCHISE BUSINESS

There are many advantages to buying a franchise business, especially a well-known one, rather than building a business from scratch. A disadvantage of owning a franchise is that you will not have the satisfaction of saying, "This business was my idea." However, the main reason for starting your own business is to make money and gain independence, and you are more likely to succeed with a franchise than with a business idea of your own.

One of the key advantages of buying a franchise is that you hit the ground running. There is no need, as with a new and unknown business, to invest heavily in building awareness of your products and services. Most franchises, even lesser-known ones, have achieved this already at a local if not the national level. Most people are already aware of what the business has to offer and provided it is a popular franchise, are "prepped" to feel positive about your business.

Another advantage of buying a franchised business is that you can do things the right way - the way that works - from day one. Typically, it takes several years for a new business to find its feet in terms of what works and what doesn't. Mistakes cost money. When you buy a franchise you also buy an entire system of practices, procedures, and policies that are a proven formula for success. In other words, you can start making money right away instead of losing it on the learning curve.

When you buy a franchise, owners and staff receive valuable training from the franchise which ensures your business meets customer expectations from the start. Again, this enables you to avoid a costly learning curve and immediately capitalize on the popularity of your franchise.

Another advantage to buying a franchise is that there is no need to spend a fortune on advertising and promotions. Firstly, your business is already well-known. Secondly, the franchise will supply all the necessary signage. Thirdly, franchisers often run major campaigns which individual outlets could never afford. All you need to do is spend what you need to spend to keep the customers coming and build on existing popularity.

A final advantage - and it is an important one - is that by buying a franchise you are buying an easy option for independence. Despite initial excitement and enthusiasm, the stresses and strains of starting a business from scratch, with little or no support, often prove too much for new business owners. Once again, the purpose of owning your own business is essential to gain ownership of your own life. As you can see, given the choice between your own idea for a business - risky and costly in more ways than one - there are clear advantages to buying a franchise business.

BENEFITS OF BEING PART OF FRANCHISING OVER STARTING FROM SCRATCH

Owning your own business is an attractive prospect for many people, but it does carry a great deal of risk with it. There are many advantages to working within a franchise rather than starting your own business.

Being part of a franchise gives a greater sense of security for the business owner, as you have the backing of a much larger parent company behind you. They can give you access to professional business advice, training, and resources not normally available for your traditional business owner.

PRIMARY BENEFITS

1.   LEARN TO RUN THE BUSINESS EFFECTIVELY:

Being part of a franchise team gives you access to mentoring and advice from those that know how to run a business effectively. You will be able to use a tried and trusted formula when running that franchise and have confidence that it is a winning model.

Even if you lack experience in specific facets of a business, owning a franchise will allow you to plug these knowledge gaps and gain the required skills quickly.

2.   LOW BUSINESS RISK:

It is in the interest of the parent company for the individual franchise to succeed. For this reason, there is a dramatically lower risk involved than when starting a company from scratch. Franchise businesses have a 2-3 times greater chance of success than other small businesses starting up.

3.   REDUCED RUNNING COSTS:

As a member of a franchise group you can benefit from the bulk buying power of the parent company and save money on day-to-day running costs. If you are keen on starting up your own company, make sure you research the possibility of a franchise business first.

4.   REPUTATION BUILDING:

Trading under an already established name will take a lot of the work out of brand and reputation building, which can take a significant chunk of your marketing budget, especially initially.

5.   A BUSINESS MODEL:

While starting your own business means you will have to learn and form everything from scratch, franchising offers you a working business model for running a business. Franchising is a network of interdependent business relationships that allows a number of people to share a brand identification, a successful method of doing business, and a strong marketing and distribution system.

6.   SAFETY IN PROVEN SYSTEMS:

For the franchisee, franchising is about risk reduction and safety. You trade in the freedom associated with being an independent owner for an opportunity to become part of a group of people committed to building a brand and dominating markets using a common,   tested   operating   system.

No more guesswork about the most effective way to build your business: The franchise provides a proven method (the operating system), a brand or trademark recognized by customers, and technical support so you won't have to reinvent the wheel to be successful.

On the other hand, you provide the capital to expand the brand faster than the franchise can by itself as well as the management talent to run the business and execute the operating system.

7.   PREDICTABLE RESULTS:

Being part of a franchise system should also provide group buying power to cut your operating expenses, faster growth due to tested marketing programs, predictable results based on your adherence to the operating system and less risk of your invested capital. The trade-offs for you are the fees you pay the franchise for the operating license and the restrictions imposed by the franchise on the method of operating the business.

THE BOTTOM LINE

The bottom line is whether you would like to run your business your own way or own a well-known branch while adhering to a working business model with rules set by someone else. Your answer to this question will tell you whether franchising is for you.

ADVANTAGES OF STARTING YOUR BUSINESS FROM SCRATCH

Starting a business of your own with an idea, and a bit of imagination allows you to be your own boss. Starting a business can be a difficult decision if you are not sure if you have what it really takes to be an entrepreneur. Don't worry; everyone starting out, in building any type of business has those same thoughts to some degree.

First, you should think about how you can start a business. You can start a business from scratch, and this means without buying any idea or model that is already established. This is one of the riskiest paths to self-employment, but one that many have done successfully in the past. It may also be the most satisfying and fulfilling should you succeed. Every day new restaurants, retail outlets, stores, service centers and the like are being established, fresh and new to the market. This is your clean slate, where you can start your own reputation; your own name in the industry, and you put forth your own thoughts and ideas into the business world.

The advantage to your own start-up business is you will learn from your mistakes, making changes along the way. If you were to hire the wrong type of employees, or if you have the wrong location, you can change these things. You make the decisions; no set patterns or ideas you must follow to get additional sales for your business.

Although, building a business is a challenge. There is much to learn and overcome. Nevertheless, it can be very rewarding both personally and financially. Knowing why you want to start a business in the first place can help you stay focused and keep you moving forward through adversity.

BY STARTING YOUR OWN BUSINESS, YOU:

1.	ACQUIRE NEW SKILLS:

Starting a business from scratch offers you the opportunity for constant and never-ending improvement. It allows you to enhance and acquire new skills like marketing, management, productivity, communication, delegation, research, product development, technical skills, and a variety of others. Although this can be overwhelming at times, the effect is that you are better prepared for uncertainty and change because you have worked to broaden your skill sets and knowledge. As a result, you have more options at your disposal. This is particularly important in a dynamic and uncertain world.

2.	SHARPEN YOUR CREATIVITY:

To start a business from scratch, you must use the power of your mind to create. Whether you create an actual product, marketing materials, training for your team, come up with new strategies, try new techniques, and so on, a business will force you to sharpen your creativity and become more innovative. It is just a natural process of engaging in a productive endeavor. The more you apply your mind to a creative project, the more you will build your creative thinking muscles.

3.   BUILD YOUR OWN ASSETS:

Starting a business from scratch gives you the unique ability to create assets that you own. Whether it is a product, a service, intellectual property, or a brand, your business is an asset that has value and can potentially generate income for years to come. You can, in turn, reinvest the income you generate into enhancing your skill sets, growing your business, or purchasing other income producing assets. There is something very powerful about creating and owning your own assets. Starting your own business gives you the means to do that.

4.   IDENTIFY AND SOLVE PROBLEMS:

The purpose of a business is to solve problems and satisfy the needs, wants, and desires of others. Starting your own business forces you to become more observant and identify the problems that people face on a daily basis. As a business owner, you now have an incentive to solve problems and meet people's needs.

The more you practice identifying problems and coming up with solutions, the better you become at this process. As a result, the better you become at serving others through your business.

5.   OFFER YOUR OWN PRODUCTS AND SERVICES THAT SERVE THE COMMUNITY:

Through your business, you have the privilege of making a positive impact in the lives of others. By providing value through your products and/or services, you have the potential to help solve people's problems and meet their needs. A lot of satisfaction can be derived from knowing that you are making a positive contribution to the lives others by serving them through your products and services. This is yet another appealing reason to start your own business from scratch.

Now that you have become aware of more reasons to start a business from scratch, the next step becomes how to get started. Of course, there are many ways to go about doing this. One of the easiest and fastest ways to get started is to use a simple marketing system that has already been created. The advantage of using such a system is that you don't have to invest the time or the money to create another one. You can simply focus on learning marketing skills and generating an income right away while you develop more advanced skills and clarify exactly what you want to focus on in the meantime. You can then take the income that you generate and reinvest it into your business education and the tools you need to grow your business even further.

Whether you choose to franchise a business or start from scratch, that doesn't mean you always have to stick with that one business model forever. The way we become financially independent is to have multiple strams of income. Many franchise owners dabble in multiple business ideas once their franchised business is on auto pilot. Many "start from scratch" business owners learn the do's and don'ts of owning a business the hard way through mistakes, thus making a franchise opportunity a walk in the park for them.

CHAPTER THREE

STARTING YOUR OWN BUSINESS: DO IT RIGHT

WHAT ARE YOU GOOD AT? WHAT DO YOU LIKE?

It is perhaps the true "American Dream" to leave your job working for someone else and start your own business? The idea is that not only do you have more control over your time commitment, pay, and the types of customers you deal with - but it also enables people to engage in an activity they actually have a passion for. However, just having that passion is not enough to make a venture successful. It takes thorough planning and a major time investment.

1.   CHOOSE SOMETHING THAT YOU HAVE A PASSION FOR:

This venture is still a job, and you will be less likely to put forth the requisite effort and care if you are not emotionally attached to the business.

2.   DO YOUR RESEARCH INTO THE MARKET YOU ARE LOOKING TO GET INTO:

Unless you have a new invention or can revolutionize a current process, you need to find a niche market in which you can differentiate yourself from every other similar business.

3.   ALWAYS CONSULT A LEGAL PROFESSIONAL:

Preferably one that specializes in business start-ups or an accounting professional. They will be the best source of guidance when it comes to selecting a business structure and naming issues, as well as state and local licensing issues.

4.   STICK TO WHAT YOU KNOW BEST AND DO NOT TRY TO DO EVERYTHING YOURSELF:

If you are not good at handling finances, then hire an accountant or bookkeeper. If you are not graphically inclined, then hire a design firm to create your logo and marketing tools. It is always cheaper to spend the money and have it done right from the beginning than it is to fix a problem over and over again.

5.   DO NOT RUSH:

Take your time and make sure that everything is to your specification. You need to be100% ready for business from the day the doors first open.

6.   NETWORK.

Tell everyone you know about your business. Word of mouth is the cheapest and most effective form of marketing. Also, solicit their opinions on everything from the name of the business, to the logo design, to the promotions you will be having. Having outsiders who are less biased critique your business leads to more honest reviews and will most likely reflect the public's opinion as well.

7. Make sure to budget enough money for advertising & marketing, as well as overhead, legal & accounting, insurance, etc.

8. Have patience. Success is not an overnight occurrence and generally will take much time, work, and effort.

9. Talk to people who are successful in the industry you are looking to enter (although try to choose people who you will not be in

direct competition with). Try to pick their brains as much as you can without being intrusive. Many successful people are more than happy to share their stories and how the got to where they are.

10. Join professional associations suh as the local Chamber of Commerce and networking groups. Form strategic alliances with others who offer similar yet distinctive products or services to gain mutual benefit.

11. Don't be afraid to take calculated risks; just don't be reckless. There's no reward without risk, but don't take that risk without weighing the pros and cons first.

Above all else, surround yourself with positive people who will support you and your ideas.

This list is by no means complete, and in my estimation can never be considered complete. There are too many things that need consideration, and everything varies by experience level and industry. However, this is a good starting point.

WHAT ARE YOU GOOD AT? WHAT DO YOU LIKE?

Step 1: MAKE UP YOUR MIND:

It all starts here. Decide that you're ready: Say "I'm ready to run my own business." Find a spot in your house or rent/lease a location. Pick a day on your calendar.

Step 2: PICK AN AREA

Maybe right this minute you have no idea what to do. That's fine. Keep looking; just don't take a decade doing it. The best place to start is, of course, your hobby. Turn your hobby of scrapbooking, soap making, or model trains into a profit. You're not the only one with this interest. In this day and age, you can find a niche market in almost anything. Use your hobby as a business idea.

Step 3: MAKE IT LEGAL

Now, this is the part that often deters many aspiring entrepreneurs; don't let it! Your government wants you to run your own business and have set up tremendous incentives for you. The Small Business Association (SBA) provides a "Starting Your Business" section of their website that can give everything you need to know about the legal aspects of starting a business.

One last food for thought: Experts believe that the next wave of millionaires is likely to be dominated by small-business entrepreneurs; you can be one of them.

FINDING THE PERFECT IDEA

The answer to this question is that the perfect idea probably doesn't exist. Your aim should be to choose an idea that is practical and workable, given your skills and experience, and your long-term goals. It should also be an idea that fires your enthusiasm and something that you can really believe in! Charles J. Duell, the Commissioner of the US patent office in 1899 once said "Everything that can be invented has already been invented". Boy, was he wrong... The same thing has probably been said today once or twice, and it would still be just as wrong.

Some new business owners find it hard to settle on a single business idea because they are worried about missing out on new opportunities or narrowing their options too early on. But remember, even when you have started your business, it is possible to add new services or products, or even to begin a second or third business.

You and your businesses will continue to grow and develop - so in selecting your first business idea, you are not saying 'no' to other opportunities. However, to give your first business idea a really strong start you might need to put other ideas on hold for a while, or at least on the back burner. Your current business model deserves your undivided attention at all times. Don't get distracted by the "shiny objects". By shiny objects, I mean the next big craze in the business world, the too good to be true niche, the next profitable venture or pyramid scheme. Don't do it. Be completely devoted to one idea at a time until it works or doesn't work.

THE INSPIRATION FOR YOUR NEW BUSINESS MAY COME FROM:

a. INVENTING SOMETHING NEW:

Some people are naturally good at finding original solutions to problems. Others come up with completely new ideas based on new technology or other developments. Sometimes people are driven to invent a solution when they are faced with a problem in their own life and realize there is no solution... yet.

b. TWEAKING SOMEONE ELSES IDEA TO MAKE IT BETTER:

This can be a great starting point. If an idea is working for one business, there's a good chance it could work for yours too.

However, this one needs to be handled with care. If the marketplace is already overcrowded, you will need to offer something really special to earn your share of customers.

c. SPOTTING A GAP IN THE MARKET:

This often happens by accident. Perhaps you look everywhere for something you need, only to realize that no one in your area is providing it.

d. DEVELOPING YOUR OWN SKILLS AND INTERESTS:

Building on your own areas of expertise can be a great starting point, because you probably already understand the market and the needs of your potential customers quite well. Many people dream of earning a living doing something they love, and there is no reason why they shouldn't achieve this goal, given careful planning and hard work. Business ideas may be found in the most unexpected places or in everyday situations. Ideas don't need to be wildly inventive or original to succeed.

Ultimately your idea is only a good one if it allows you to create a sustainable business. It is important to assess your ideas objectively in the cold light of day. By all means, seek expert opinionsa and ask the opinions of people you trust. But make your own assessment of the facts as well. Business history is littered with examples of highly successful business ideas that no one but their inventor believed would work.

Thorough market research is critical - it can tell you whether customers really are willing to buy your product or service. It can also give you a good idea of what you should be charging and reveal who your competitors are.

Carrying out the following key steps will reveal whether you have a viable idea or not. At best they will give you a solid launch pad for your business; at worst they will reveal an unobtainable hurdle that causes you to seek out alternative ideas. But if there is a major problem, it is better to identify it now than six months down the line when you have already invested time, money and emotional energy into your idea.

CHAPTER FOUR

PICKING THE RIGHT NICHE WHEN STARTING YOUR OWN BUSINESS

One of the biggest mistakes you can make when starting your own business is picking the wrong niche. Picking the wrong niche can be detrimental to the success of your business and you may find it nearly impossible to make any money if you haven't done your research.

If you pick a niche that isn't hot you are setting yourself up for failure.

In picking the right niche:

a. List all the skills you have.

b. Think about the experiences you've gained in your work and personal life. List the most significant.

c. List any other hobbies and interests you have.

d. Ask your friends and family for their impressions of your greatest strengths and skills. Ask them to tell you honestly what they think your weakest points are in terms of setting up your own business.

e. Look out for gaps in the market.

f. Explore other businesses and identify those you might be able to build off of. Look for ways in which you can improve on the business in question. What can you offer that they do not? How can the product or service be improved?

Now, work through the following, and jot down your answer to each question:

a. What is it that you will personally bring to the business in terms of relevant experience and expertise? In what way are you qualified to run this particular business?

b. Just as importantly, are there any skills or is there any knowledge that you need to acquire before you can run this business?

c. Is there a market - a need for the idea and customers who will pay for it?

d. How big is the market, and how will you reach it?

e. Who are your main competitors?

f. How will you fund your business? (How much income do you need?)

g. What might go wrong?

It will also help if you keep up-to-date with the current events to help you identify new trends and new products being launched.

ALSO, INVESTIGATE THE MARKETPLACE THOROUGHLY.

IDENTIFY YOUR CUSTOMERS AND GET TO KNOW THEIR LIKES AND

DISLIKES.

Identify your competitors - how many of them are there, and how successful are they? Who is the lead player? Who is second? Find out as much as you can about them - collect brochures, marketing material and any other information you can. Test out their websites and call their customer service number or visit their shop or office if it is open to the public. Analyze their service or product honestly and objectively. What are their strengths? What are their weaknesses?

How much is it going to cost to launch your business (that is to get the first product on the shelf, to serve the first customer or to provide your service for your first client)?

WHERE IS THE MONEY GOING TO COME FROM?

Include money in your plan for contingencies. Consider what might go wrong - not just financially, but in other ways too such as legally, emotionally, physically. Plan for the unexpected and think through both the best and worst-case scenarios.

ASSESS YOUR BUSINESS'S LONG-TERM POTENTIAL.

Visualize yourself running your business. All this is necessary to pick the right niche.

CHAPTER FIVE
HOW TO FIND INVESTORS

Finding an investor for your business provides you with the seed money you may need to start the business. In return for investing in your business, most investors receive a percentage of the sales or company stock. Finding an investor for your business may be harder than it sounds, but there are a few ways to go about locating and convincing investors to invest in your business.

A good team of investors can play a great role in the success of your business, but a bad choice of investors can obliterate even the strongest ideas and business plans. Believe it or not, investors provide more opportunities to your business, while becoming resources for creating effective marketing ideas. Knowing what to consider while selecting investors and being able to attract the right type of investors are vital skills for established and emerging entrepreneurs. They want you to succeed just as much as you do, and often times offer more resources than just startup capital.

If you are a small business owner and finding trouble convincing investors, here are some secrets that will help you attract the eye of an angel investor or venture capital, while making your business a more appealing investment.

1.   GET THE MOST OUT OF NETWORKING

Networking is the best way for entrepreneurs to pitch their startup in a less formal and organic way. If you are building a great business, networking within the local startup and investing community can be the best way to meet and find the right type of investors. If you find investors interested in your business, keep the meetings going and let things happen organically for optimum results. Let them consider your business; after all, you are not only conveying your idea, you are actually relying on the social capital built through the networking process that impacts the investment decision.

2.   BE PRACTICAL, GET REAL PAYING CUSTOMERS

You need investment to attract customers, but you need customers to acquire money. It is always worth it to make an effort to get customers prior to approaching an investor, instead of seeking funds first and customers second. It is advised to create a plan to acquire customers first that doesn't need a very large investment.

This is very important, particularly for emerging entrepreneurs; it will become easier to get investors on good terms. Investors always want proof that your idea is effective enough and will work, and nothing will satisfy them than having real paying users.

3.   FIND THE RIGHT CO-FOUNDER

When you find investors, you are not only selling them your business in terms of products and services, you are selling them on your team. Opting for the right leadership team for your small business is an important process and having the wrong co-founders can be more dangerous for your business than having no co-founder at all. However, finding the right co-founder can make the process easier, even beyond attracting investors. As having partners will allow you to rely on them, which can be a huge boost for your startup.

4.   GET A BETTER RETURN ON INVESTMENT (ROI)

Though investors may start believing in your business, the purpose of their investment is to make money. Therefore, it is important to highlight what they will actually gain from investing in your startup. No matter if you are approaching an angel, VC or a rich entrepreneur, it is important to show how you are going to obtain their investment return. It is alluring to focus on yourself and your business vision, but at the end of the day, investors want to know what is in it for them. Therefore, the best way to stand out and get interest is to clearly explain how and when they will see a return.

5.   TAKE BENEFIT OF THE ONLINE FUNDRAISING MARKET

Networking is important, but your location should not be the restricting factor when it comes to securing an investment. There are different fundraising platforms available and you are no longer restricted to only being able to raise money. If your company has best-in-class metrics for your industry, you should be able to double your money. Post your business's best metrics and find investors on the platform related to your industry.

6.   PICK THE RIGHT INVESTOR

In order to attract the attention of the right investor, make sure your product solves real problems. Many entrepreneurs only attempt to reinvent the wheel; therefore, it is advised to highlight the qualities of your product to attract the real investors. Doing so will get users and revenue. Think outside the box and do something useful.

7.   GRADUATING FROM A TOP ACCELERATOR

Emerging and first-time entrepreneurs are advised to apply to reputable startup accelerators that will lead their credibility to your company. Joining an accelerator can be helpful for rising startups. Though it doesn't guarantee that you will attract investors, it does make your startup a more appealing investment candidate. Graduating from a reputable accelerator doesn't guarantee funding, but can greatly improve the chances that you would raise a favorable valuation.

8. WRITE A BUSINESS PLAN

Before looking for investors, write a business plan. A business plan is a written guide to your business including the purpose, the startup costs, expenses, sales forecasts and other information to gain the interest of investors.

9. MAKE A LIST OF POSSIBLE INVESTORS

Add people you know to the list who have money to invest and may be willing to take a risk with your business startup. Friends, family members and business owners of related businesses are the best places to start. For example, if your business involves a computer software product, then other software companies may be interested in investing in your company.

10. DEVELOP AN INVESTOR PRESENTATION

Compile a speech or pitch to present the business idea for convincing investors to invest in your startup. Include information in your presentation that includes what the product or service offering for the business is, the costs involved in starting the business, what kind of demand there is in the market for the product or service and how much the company stands to make in one year, three years and so on.

11.   CONTACT THE POSSIBLE INVESTORS

Schedule a time to meet with and make your presentation to each investor on your list.

12.   PRESENT YOUR BUSINESS IDEA TO INVESTORS

At the meeting with the investor(s), pitch your business by giving your presentation and providing a copy of your business plan. Answer any questions the investor has about the startup and tell the investor what is in for them such as shares of the company stock or a percentage of the sales. This is an interview; sell yourself and the company.

13.   SIGN AN INVESTOR AGREEMENT

Once you find an investor, put your agreement in writing. You can find general agreement templates online or work with a business attorney to help you draw up a legally binding contract for both you as the business owner and the investor to sign.

CHAPTER SIX

TAKE YOUR BUSINESS ONLINE, EVEN IF IT'S NOT INTERNET BASED

It is best for you to take advantage of what advanced technology has in store for you. The internet has opened for you a far wider access to more clients, distributors, and investors.

There are many of reasons why it is a good idea to take your business online, to name few:

1. ENHANCE BUSINESS CREDIBILITY

Nowadays, with the internet revolution, if your business does not exist online, it is more prone to losing credibility and competition in the market place.

2. ENHANCE PR

Having 24/7 access to important information about your business, contact info, product lists, etc... is a very powerful PR tool that your business can benefit from. Also, having free useful information for your clients' knowledge enrichment makes your website a valuable community resource; this means that more traffic will be driven to your website.

3. INCREASE PROFIT

Having more online traffic leads to more profit. Every year more and more people are making purchases online as opposed to walking into a store. It's easier, cheaper, and safer in terms of going to a store.

4. EVERYONE, EXCEPT YOU, IS DOING BUSINESS ONLINE

You've been left behind and that's why you feel that your business is not picking up. Before closing your doors or trying a new idea, try enlisting the help of a friend or a business partner on how to make your business online accessible. If not, you can surf the internet and find a company that will help you set up the system for an online business. These companies charge affordable prices in lieu for doing each and every detail for you.

5. YOU GET THE KNOWLEDGE ABOUT THE LATEST TECHNOLOGY

Sayng that the internet is the most effective medium by which people can get and process information is an understatement. For some people, it is the only right medium by virtue of the internet's speed and volume of materials for knowledge.

Being a business individual, you don't have any other tool that will help you succeed mores than the internet. From human resource management to incorporating new techniques in improving your operations and your product, the internet is ready to give you what you need.

6. YOU GET A WIDER ACCESS TO CLIENTS FROM BOTH IN-STORE AND ONLINE

You do not want to run a small business that doesn't allow you to come up with new products and services to offer. Online businesses can be accessed by more people all over the world. Everyone is doing their transactions online and you really have to accommodate the growing demand for products among people. If you cannot be accessed online, people will think that your business does not exist.

7. YOU SAVE TIME WHEN YOU TAKE YOUR BUSINESS ONLINE

Recent research findings have shown that people can save time and money as much as 60% percent of the time when transactions are done online. The Internet offers the fastest venue for communication among people apart from the faster mode of exchange of goods and services. For you, that is a way of finding time for you and your family.

8. Your money is safer when transactions are done online provided you take precautionary measures against scammers. Keep those passwords and important numbers in your head and do not share them with anybody. With an online business, there will be no checks to sign and no cash to take to the bank.

9. GET MORE SATISFIED CUSTOMERS

An online presence will allow you to provide your customers or prospects with immediate answers to their questions without them waiting for your physical storefront to open, being placed on hold, or awaiting delivery of your company brochure. Saving your customers time, in turn, saves you the exorbitant cost of print advertising design, manufacture and mailing - and possibly the cost of losing your prospect during the wait.

10. REDUCE OPERATING COSTS

You can sell your products and services online and automate responses to customers without the need for additional sales or customer service staff.

11. MINIMAL INVESTMENT, HIGHER RETURNS

Whether you build your website yourself, purchase a low-cost template or get a custom design by a professional designer, a successful website produces a higher return on investment than any other medium. Consider the cost of a website compared to the expense of an ad in the Yellow Pages (that nobody reads anyways), print marketing materials or the additional staff required to offer round-the-clock service, and you'll find that a website can offer your business greater exposure, savings and profit potential than other methods for only a fraction of the price.

Taking your business online and promoting it regularly may dramatically increase your sales and get you ready for other big plans and promotions. It's a great way to encourage and engage your customers. Now the question is, when are you going to take your business online?

BUILD A BRAND

Small businesses get started in a variety of ways. Most small businesses have gone through the rigor of developing a business plan. However, the really successful small businesses also think about how to build a brand, not just a business. Your brand communicates who you are and what you do as a business. It helps you stand out from competitors in your market. It represents a promise to your customers that when they buy your product or service, they will receive a certain value every time.

When most people think of branding, they think of logos, taglines, value propositions, advertising slogans, and other common branding tools. But there's a lot of different ways to build a brand.

TO BUILD BRAND:

1. BUILD A BRAND WITH DISTINCTION

It is critical to be distinctive if you want to build a brand. Let's be honest and admit that few small businesses offer something that no one ever thought of before. So, how do you make yourself attractive to your customers? You must create a distinct and engaging brand personality. Your brand should be the person your customer wants to do business with.

You want to be memorable and stand for something. You must be distinctive enough that you can build a brand. Otherwise, you will just be another supplier in the category.

2. BUILD A BRAND WITH CONSISTENCY

Once you've created this distinct brand personality, you must be consistent. The only way to build a brand is to stay with the message. Small businesses frequently chase everything that gets in front of them. Avoid the tendency to become reactionary. Stay true to your message with your personality. It is the repetition and consistency that will build a brand for you.

Small business owners frequently get tired of their own brand long before the customer does. Just because you are bored with something doesn't mean it isn't working or that your customers are bored too. You live with your brand everyday, your customers probably don't. So don't fall into the trap of change for the sake of change. If you want to build a strong brand it will take time.

3.   BUILD A BRAND BY EVOLVING

There will be times when you need to change. Make certain that you evolve the brand. Listen to your customers. Their perception of your brand is your reality. Keep the brand fresh and relevant but true to your original core values. After all, those values are what made you stand out in the first place.

Don't lose that. Evolution is part of building a brand.

4.   BUILD A BRAND WITH GUTS

To build a brand you must also embrace it. Don't be afraid of what it is. Don't pull your punches. Sometimes to be true to the brand you built you might not be attractive to another part of the marketplace. If you water your brand down so that it includes everyone, you probably don't stand for anything. Don't water down your niche and become too broad. You can't please everyone.

ALSO, BUILD YOUR BRAND WITH:

6. INTERIOR DESIGN: The way your place of business looks on the inside sends a powerful message about your commitment to the business. Is your interior neat, clean, and professional? This goes the same for online websites as well.

Does it make clients feel welcome when they walk through the door? Does it reflect the look and feel that clients expect from your type of business? Investing in interior design shows that you are serious about the business and plan to be around for a long time. By itself, the interior design probably won't cause a prospect to do business with you. However, it can definitely swing their decision in the right (or wrong) direction.

7. PERSONAL BRANDING: As head of the business, you are your company's leading brand ambassador. Which means everything you think, do and say contributes to your brand. The way you dress, your posture, the way you speak - these all play a role in shaping customers' perceptions about the value of doing business with you. There are many ways to develop your personal brand, but the key is to make sure it aligns with your company's brand. If you're selling tailored suits, you had better look like a million bucks.

8. PARTIES AND SOCIAL EVENTS: As a business owner, you're on even when you're off. At non-work parties and social events, you're still representing your business. This gives you an excellent opportunity to build your brand. Parties allow you to meet new people, reconnect with those you already know, and identify people who could be clients, strategic partners or referral sources. Hosting a party or event doubles the opportunity, as it obligates you to interact with all the guests.

9. YOUR CAR: Your business may not lend itself to such a campy look or humorous approach. But with a little ingenuity, your car may help to build your brand every time you drive it.

10. YOUTUBE VIDEOS: Creating your own YouTube channel and videos offers an inexpensive and very effective way to build your brand. Videos can include everything from "verbal" white papers to customer testimonials, industry thought leadership and more.

Today's viewers expect videos with high production quality, so don't post anything that looks sloppy, cheap, or homemade.

Everything you do as a business contributes to your brand - the purpose of which is to define, differentiate and communicate your unique value proposition. Never try to imitate another brand. Instead, get creative about your own brand, and build your brand communications around what will hit home with your customers or clients. So go ahead and be who you are.

If you've done your homework you will have your audience. Others will find you attractive because you stick to your core values. It's okay if some people don't like who you are as a brand. That means you stand for something. Again, you can't please everyone.

CHAPTER SEVEN

COMMON MISTAKES MADE BY NEW BUSINESS OWNERS

Most new small businesses won't be in business this time next year. That's the cold hard truth behind it. Though it is easy to start your own business, it takes a lot more to succeed in business. There are common mistakes made by small business owners. Let's explore them so you can avoid them.

1.   NEGLECTING YOUR CONTINUING EDUCATION

You are the only renewable resource, besides your employees, your business has. You may be a master at getting the most out of your other resources, but how are you doing with you?

Today's world is characterized by rapid change. Keeping up on innovations in your business and new business strategies is crucial for long-term success. However, most small business owners do not invest any time or money into developing themselves. The less you know, the more time, money and energy you will waste employing others who do.

2.   UNREALISTIC EXPECTATIONS

There's an old saying in business that says you can have things fast, good, or affordable. It goes on to state that the best you can usually do is two out of three so decide which two are most important to you and go forward from there. Fast and affordable may not be good, and fast and good will probably cost you more than you'd like to pay. Expecting all three each and every time may be, well, unrealistic.

3.   FAILING TO PLAN IS PLANNING TO FAIL

Many small business owners avoid planning at all costs. The old adage, "Failing to plan is planning to fail", is true. Without a well-thought out plan for establishing your business, running your business, and marketing your business, you will waste a lot of time. The time you don't have.

So, how do we find time to plan while we're trying to run a business? Do the work in small increments. Keep a notebook handy throughout your day. Have sections designated for "Operations", "Finance", and "Marketing". Make notes as random thoughts appear to you during the day. At the end of each week, take an hour or so and summarize the ideas into a plan. Place the actions that will yield the highest potential return at the top of the list. Start Monday of the next week by tackling the items at the top of your list.

4.   ALL WORK AND NO PLAY

Running your own business is hard work. There is no doubt about that. However, without proper relaxation, you will become increasingly less productive. It isn't the hours you spend at work but the productivity of the hours you spend there. Become a student of your own business. When do most customers access your business? When is the slow time of the day or week? If you are available for an entire hour that may only yield one small sale, you may be better off out of the office.

Take a walk. Talk to people along the way. They could be future customers. Join a gym and work out during half of that slow hour. This kills two birds with one stone. You become healthier with better endurance and again, you can network with people who might be future customers.

5.   TAKE YOUR EXISTING CUSTOMERS FOR GRANTED

Remember the first customer you ever had? Remember the appreciation you had for them? Remember the little things you did for them? When did you stop and WHY?

Avoid looking after your existing customers and they will go elsewhere. Customers have more options today than they ever had before. If they don't find your competitor locally, they will find them on the Internet. Ignore customers at your own expense.

The fact is without them you wouldn't be in business. It's time to make certain they understand how much you really appreciate them. How about having a special reception or buffet on site for your customers? What about a special appreciation day?

When was the last time you contacted customers just to tell them how much you appreciate their business? A happy customer is a valuable business asset, now and in the future.

6.   NEVER ASK FOR REFERRALS

As stated above, your existing, happy customers are a major business asset. That asset can yield benefits in many ways. But you have to ask. Instead of spending a lot of money on your advertising, why not ask customers for referrals? Referral sales are the cheapest and easiest way to grow your business.

7.   ONE-STOP SHOP MENTALITY

Many business owners fail to achieve their true potential because they try to be all things to all people. You need to target your ideal customers. Look at your product. Ask yourself who would benefit most from your product. Once you have selected a targeted group, learn everything you can about them.

Change your store or website to reflect that targeted customer's needs and desires. Speak their language. Find out where they hang out and what they read or listen to. Understand their concerns. Sell them solutions, not products, and you will excel!

8.   NEGLECTING MARKETING

It is so easy for a business owner to get caught up in the daily operations of a business. The inventory ordering, order processing, data input, hiring and more, can become all-consuming. Then one day you look up and wonder what happened to the business.

Marketing is all about future sales. You plant the seed today to reap the benefits tomorrow. If you want a long-term successful business you can hand off to your children or sell for retirement, don't neglect marketing. Every month, set aside at least 20% of your time dedicated to marketing activities.

Marketing activities include deciding to expand an existing product line, dumping unprofitable products or adding new products. Determine where your advertising can generate the biggest return on the investment and plan out your marketing process. These are crucial functions for your success. Again, neglect them at your own expense!

9.   THINKING YOU DON'T NEED A BUSINESS PLAN

Yes, you do! Business plans force you to examine your concept, study the competition, think about costs and plan a long-term winning strategy. A business plan is most often used to seek start-up funding, proving to the lender that the business will succeed. Even if you don't need funding, taking the time to plan your business before running it is the smartest step you can make towards long-term success.

10.   MENTAL BOOKKEEPING

Keeping "the books" all in your head is a great way to get into big financial trouble. Expenses and income need to be carefully documented. Suppliers, customers, and the IRS aren't going to accept "oh, it was about $3500, give or take" when they come to you looking for a receipt.

There are many different ways to keep your books. If you prefer not to track of your finances with pencil and paper, try one of the many bookkeeping software packages available. If you still feel that you can't keep on top of making timely entries, hire a bookkeeper or accountant to keep all your business finances in order. You will be glad you did.

11.   SPENDING MONEY YOU DIDN'T NEED TO SPEND

Don't blow through all your startup capital. If you've done your business plan as you should, you will understand your break-even point. Budget carefully so that your business can operate beyond that point. Expect the unexpected and be prepared for sudden market changes, late-paying customers or other unforeseen expenses beyond your control. Don't fall into the trap of buying into the latest fad or gimmick before thoroughly checking it out.

12.   LACK OF BALANCE

While starting and running your own business requires a lot of hard work and dedication, ignoring loved ones can be as detrimental to your emotional and physical health as the business failing.

Make sure that family and close companions understand and accept that you'll be working long hours to get your dream off the ground. By the same token, make sure that you don't abandon them. There are some life experiences that are not repeatable. Take the time off to enjoy them.

13.   COMMON MISCONCEPTIONS

You just need a great idea or technology. There is no such thing as the "perfect idea" – only how you implement it. Everyone has great ideas, the trick is to tap into a market need and create a winning product or service that solves a problem or a need. Many ventures hire their technical talent; the leader has a vision of the market that leads to success. You understand the market because you have talked to a few friends. Thorough market research is required to know who will buy, and why, to determine what characteristics will cause your product or service to appeal. If you can't answer, "what problem does this solve", then you don't have a viable business idea. You have no competitors. All businesses have competitors because anyone can choose to spend their money on something else, even if it isn't the same as what you are doing or developing.

14.   NOT PLANNING FOR GROWTH

All entrepreneurs want to grow their business. They want to be in a situation where progressive steps toward becoming a larger organization happen daily. Often though, many small business IT systems were not purchased with the intention or potential for growth. This can be for a variety of reasons, lack of knowledge, budgetary limitations, or even failure to plan effectively. No matter the reason, the lack of scalability can lead to a very cost ineffective repeat purchasing of technology.

15.   NO PLAN FOR SOCIAL MEDIA MARKETING

There is currently a huge buzz about the business benefits of social media. So much so that business owners rushed to get online and have their websites optimized for search engines several years ago. Businesses all over the world are frantically trying to establish a presence on sites like Twitter, Facebook, Google Plus and LinkedIn. Countless businesses have figured out how best to use these sites and are already reaping massive rewards.

However, many are floundering too because they tend to make certain types of mistakes.

Sadly, many business owers are seduced by the numbers. They end up buying fans and followers. Doing so is a complete waste of money. If you are in business and new to social media, it helps a lot if you can avoid making these common mistakes. The key is to log into these sites regularly and be active on them. Engage with others often. Ask compelling questions, and offer thoughtful answers.

Share, retweet, and like often. Always be friendly, helpful and polite. Slowly but surely your business will make an impact, and the benefits will accumulate.

Staying focused upon these common business mistakes can save you a lot of time and money. They are also crucial to the ongoing success of your business. Stay focused on the future while you work in the present. Don't develop work habits counterproductive to a successful outcome.

CONCLUSION

Now is the best time to start a business, launch a product or offer a cutting edge new service. More people than ever have jobs. More people than ever own homes. More business organizations are established each year than the previous year. Global prosperity is galloping along, with formerly poor countries seeing spectacular growth (potential new customers for new products and services) in the middle class.

The opportunity to successfully start a business, market an invention or new service is always dependent solely on the value, novelty, and benefits of the new offering. If there is an under-served market segment and you can identify a niche in a large market category, the time is always right to move ahead.

Time is never an entrepreneur's friend. Do not delay movement to commercialize an opportunity based on short-term business conditions, perceived or real. For example, interest rates have been historically low for the last several years. Recently they have begun to inch up. How high will they go? What effect might the rise have on the ultimate success for your venture? No one really knows the exact answer. We only can state with certainty that rates go up, rates go down. Look at the historic averages and anticipate that these averages will hold true to form. Base your financial assumptions on the mean averages, but do not delay movement on a great idea because of uncertainty about one element. Remember, if lending rates go up, they rise for your competition as well.

Also, do not listen to negative nannies nit picking your project. If you have done an effective job of due-diligence, can identify your market niche as being under-served and can quantify an excellent financial proposition, you probably have the makings of a successful business. You will certainly know more than the critics. It is easier for people to be negative than to encourage your interest in taking a risk to start your own business. Risk equates to possible failure for most people. You will be changing your life and most people instinctively fear change.

Seek advice from friends, family and valued independent counselors. It is important to know as much about your project's strengths and weaknesses as possible before committing your energy and resources.

Also know that successful entrepreneurs almost always have an inner compass which sorts through the mass of concerns, objections, and negatives they receive. It is always easier to say no and not move forward than to commit and push ahead.

America is teeming with dreamers and doers, all hoping to succeed in a cluttered, very aggressive marketplace. Delay is never a wise course of non-action if your project has real legs and commercial viability. Somebody else is potentially working on a spot on a competitive product. You cannot afford to lose your market advantage because of dallying and uncertainty about entering the market at the optimum time. There is never a perfect time to start. There is only now and now is plenty good enough. If you have a great idea and don't pursue it, I promise you will end up kicking yourself in the future for not giving it a shot. You will never know until you try.

So, what are you waiting for? Start your own business NOW and turn your dreams into a reality!

BE A BOSS

A STRAIGHT FORWARD GUIDE TO MANAGING EMPLOYEES AND GETTING THINGS DONE.

By K. Connors

INTRODUCTION

First, let's start off with a little scenario to illustrate the importance of not only good management, but the importance of hiring competent employees as well.

One afternoon, Sally told Bob, her employee, that he would be receiving some invoices in the next day or two. Sally, being the manager, sent an electronic copy of all the invoices for his reference. Now, these invoices were all from the same vendor for a particular service that had been provided to the company. Bob was required to process the approved invoices once they arrived and send payment to the vendor as usual.

About four or five days later, Bob reached out to let Sally know that he never did receive the approved invoices and furthermore, this vendor could not be paid unless they were added to the company database as a vendor/payee. Sally was furious because this particular vendor had been doing business with the company for four years and had received payment just four months prior to this occasion. She explained this to Bob, but he insisted on getting the required information to add the vendor to the database. In the end, after numerous emails and follow-ups from Sally, Bob had to apologize to for two reasons...Tthe vendor was indeed already in the company database and the invoices had been received and paid. If only Bob had spent some time researching.

Why is it that some employees can't seem to get anything right? You think back and you know you gave clear instructions but for some reason, the output does not match your request. Did you ever consider that your instructions are really not that clear? Or maybe that the employee is afraid of you and can't think straight when they have to complete a project for you? Or worse, they don't really care about their output and don't spend the time researching for accurate results. It could be any number of reasons.

CHAPTER ONE

WHAT YOU CAN DO TO HELP YOUR EMPLOYEES GET THINGS DONE RIGHT THE FIRST TIME

1. Provide detailed instructions for complex tasks: If there is no room for creativity on a task then you need to ensure that your employees know exactly what you want them to do. For example, let them know what parameters you want them to use when running a report and how you want to see the results; table, graph, chart all the above.

2. Avoid the fear factor: "Because I said so" is not a sufficient way to get through to adults. As a manager, you need to be focused on how to manage adults. It is not the same as handling children. Although, you must admit, sometimes it feels that way. Keep in mind that you want your employees to respect you rather than fear you. Respect draws out positive attitudes and results from your employees. If they respect you, they are more likely to do things correctly in order to gain your approval. They will care about their output and will ensure that they give it their best effort.

3. Train your employees to research: It's important to give your employees ample time to complete a task whenever possible. Even with a time crunch, you should encourage your employees to verify any information they compile and provide to you or anyone else within the company. They need to use the documentation you have in-house or other resources online. Teach them to realize the importance of accuracy; nobody

wants to be caught with their foot in their mouth. In Bob's case above, all he had to do was research what Sally said concerning the previous payments to the vendor.

4. Understand that you are not always right: This is true and we know it. In so many situations, employees' thoughts, suggestions and ideas are undermined as unimportant or incorrect while you as their manager expect them to take direction without question. Service and sales representatives have been taught that 'customers are always right' and that there is a proper way to agree with the customers, and then go on to correct or clear up any misconceptions they may have. In reality, you are the customer is some situations and in others, your employees are the customers. Respect each other's knowledge base and learn from each other.

There are no stupid questions. Finally, if you want something done right you have to be able to allow your employees to ask anything they need to ask to ensure that this is the case. Be patient even when the question seems silly to you - you know, those questions that make you want to say..."Are you kidding me?" Patiently reiterate what you need to be done and then let the employee handle it from there. It is better to take a deep breath and go through this step than to have the employee do the task over. Get it done right the first time.

CHAPTER TWO

THE ART OF EXECUTION

For whatever reason, execution is the greatest unaddressed issue in business today. The absence of execution is the biggest obstacle to success and often the greatest contributor to the derailment of leaders. Execution is not just tactics; it is a discipline and a system.

Leadership is not just about creating great visions, strategies, and plans. Most successful leaders are those who hold themselves accountable as well as their employees. Leaders are not successful if they cannot execute the strategy. It's like taking the time to plan a great vacation and then not taking the vacation. If you don't go on the vacation, the planning was just wasted effort. Many organizations spend significant time strategizing and planning, and very little time emphasizing execution.

Building an execution culture is not as easy as it sounds. There are many building blocks that are necessary, such as reinforcing the organization's values and understanding beliefs that influence specific behaviors in the company. However, there are some steps leaders can start implementing immediately to support better execution in the organization.

Below are strategies for instilling a culture of execution in your organization:

1.   Build accountability into meetings:

How many meetings have you attended where people left without

68

discussing who would be responsible for specific actions and by when? Begin each meeting by reviewing the status of projects or commitments from prior meetings. End each meeting by assigning specific tasks with completion dates. Assign someone to take notes and send out a recap to every member of the team.

2.   Be realistic:

Many strategies fail because leaders don't make a realistic assessment of whether the organization can execute the plan or not. Involve the management team and operational employees to ensure the plans are realistic for where the organization is right now.

3.   Focus on a few priorities:

I've seen organizations with strategic plans that detail twenty large strategies for one year. Employees (and often the executives who developed the strategies) feel so overwhelmed, that they are either paralyzed and don't take action, or do take action and fall seriously short. It's better to do a few things well than a lot of things poorly. Focus on no more than six key strategies and ensure the entire organization keeps them top of mind.

3.   Ensure employees understand priorities:

This may sound simple, but my experience is that most employees are not brought into the loop about what is important to the organization. Leaders often have a strategic plan that is kept at the executive level. Make sure the strategies are broken down and shared with employees so they know the current absolute priorities of the business.

4.   Set milestones:

Break down every organizational project into specific milestones with action items and dates. Communicate these milestones to employees and review the status at each project meeting.

5.   Use your business plan:

Is your business plan collecting dust? Many organizations go through the motions of spending two days every year developing strategic and business plans, only to stick them in the bottom of the drawer untouched. Begin by writing your business plan in simple terms with specific actionable items. Get your employees involved in the process, and review the milestones at each team meeting.

6.   Hold people at the top accountable:

If line managers are not executing, it's usually because their leader does not have an accountability structure in place. Leaders need to take ownership of their initiatives and follow-up with managers to ensure completion. Simply delegating and forgetting is not the answer. Finish every conversation with managers by summarizing the actions to be taken and setting due dates.

7.   Promote candid dialog:

This is one of the biggest reasons why things don't get done in organizations. Many managers don't want to rock the boat, so they are very polite and don't challenge each other or their leaders. This often leads to failed projects and initiatives because managers weren't honest with each other. Promote a culture of candidness.

Have each project team develop a set of agreements at the start of the project and include honest and candid dialog as an agreement.

8.   Scrutinize projects:

Most organizations start projects with a project leader and a project plan. Very few organizations make it a practice of reviewing the "lessons learned" from the project after completion. Bring the project team and stakeholders together and ask the important questions. What went well? Where did we fall short? What processes could have been better? Did we meet our time commitments? If not, why? Use this information to improve processes and hold people accountable.

9.   Confront performance issues:

Some managers put off confronting performance issues because it's unpleasant and takes time. Coach your managers to confront performance issues in a timely manner so they don't grow into bigger problems or frustrate good employees.

10.   Reward the doers:

Structure your bonus and salary increases to reward those employees who get things done. There must be enough differentiation in bonuses and salary increases to send the message that execution is rewarded.

11.   Align Systems:

Too many organizations have business units that work in silos. Everyone is working on their part, and there is no alignment of the core projects or strategies. Develop a system for ensuring the right people are involved so priorities are accomplished in a timely manner.

Holding employees accountable doesn't have to be about micro-managing or dictating. Setting clear expectations and due dates up front makes the process easier for everyone and promotes the best use of the organization's time and money.

What's the difference between leadership and management when it comes to getting things done?

Part of being a leader and/or a manager is the ability to get things done. And when I say to get things done, I am referring to the team and the way in which it responds to its leaders and managers. Although there are many areas where management and leadership overlap, there are also areas where differences can be observed. Getting things done is a classic example of this.

For a manager, getting things done can often be nothing more than informing the team of the day's goals and objectives during the morning briefing.

The manager will also guide the members of the team and help them to find the best way to achieve goals and objectives that have been set out. This is a very effective way to accomplish all kinds of goals and objectives and to keep the team involved.

Leadership, however, can have a slightly different approach. It has been said before the difference between leadership and management is that managers say "Here's what I want and this is how I want you to do it" and leaders say "Here's what I want. Now go and show me some creativity"! The idea is that leaders paint a vision of what they desire and leave it up to the group to work out how to achieve the desired result. This is, of course, a little simplistic. Any leader who merely provides a vision and then has no input at all as to how that vision is turned into a reality is being at least a little foolhardy. There has to be involvement, even if it is kept to a minimum.

The true difference lies in the way a leader lays out the vision of what he or she is trying to achieve. The word "vision" here is used deliberately as a good leader will literally conjure up an image of how the end result will look. He or she can use tools such as pictures, photos, paintings, models or good old-fashioned descriptive speech to pass on the concept of the end result to the group. He or she will not only pass that vision on, they will also pass on the level of enthusiasm that they feel towards the project or assignment.

This idea of creating a vision is something that can make a good leader stand out. There is no reason why managers can't use this technique from time to time. For everyday routine tasks, a WHAT-WHERE-WHEN can be used; but, for certain projects that are going to need to be planned out and will take some, time the idea of creating a vision in the minds of the employees and passing on that infectious enthusiasm will reap rewards.

Getting things done is a challenge that managers and leaders alike face on a day-to-day basis. Managers tend to orchestrate more while leaders tend to paint a picture and get the team to work towards it. There is no reason why managers can't utilize the qualities that make a good leader for longer projects and get the staff to show some creativity

CHAPTER THREE
KEY CHARACTERISTICS OF A GREAT BOSS

Think you have leadership qualities? Are you able to motivate others and are willing to take full responsibility of your team? If yes, you may have leadership qualities just waiting to be discovered. Depending on your working environment, you may be in a company where the chances of being discovered are low, and there is nothing as frustrating as being overlooked. If you are serious about taking your career to the next level, you need to show some initiative and not simply act on opportunities but create them instead. If your company rewards those who put themselves forward and take the lead, then show them what you are capable of. If your company does not, then show them what they are missing.

True leadership qualities are about setting objectives, whether for your own personal needs or for others who report to you. Leadership is not about feeling down in the dumps when things go wrong; it's about having the inner strength to face a challenge head on and to keep persevering if things go wrong. Having a positive attitude can make a big difference; but in business, sometimes it can be difficult to stay resilient if you make a bad decision. Taking responsibility for it, however, is vital.

People tend to be subconsciously attracted to those who convey leadership qualities and have a high level of personal value. It's important to know what makes a good leader if you want to be successful in business, networking or with any aspect of life. You must learn to convey strong leadership skills and eventually become a leader with value to offer others. People don't join a business, they join you.

Effective leadership is the result of hard work. Leaders are not born, they are made. There are many different leadership qualities because leadership is an art. So, whether you're the CEO of a Fortune 500 company or you just got promoted into a leadership position and feel a little insecure, don't worry because there's hope. Understanding the qualities of a good leader will help you sharpen your leadership skills.

Let's take a look at some powerful leadership qualities.

- Leaders of vision live believing today's dream will become tomorrow's reality. They lay out a vision before the people as a road-map to remind them where they are going.
- Creative leaders formulate the innovative ideas that promote progress and help to raise the bar. Many times, a break-through is the result of implementing a creative idea or ingenious thought.
- As you develop these leadership qualities you will have more value to offer others.
- Leaders who are trustworthy and transparent recognize integrity as a valuable asset. Long lasting relationships are built on a foundation of trust.
- Prudent leaders acknowledge their weaknesses and outsource to get the job done.
- Skillful leaders know how to handle objections and harness opposition while reaching their goals.

- Wise leaders seek counsel and consistently make wise decisions.
- Inspirational leaders fan the flame of a compelling vision in their team.
- Good character and integrity are valuable leadership qualities because of a leader's strong ability to influence.
- Courageous leaders break down the barrier of fear and take others with them.
- Leaders with insight not only see their potential but learn the skills required to unleash it.
- Accomplished leaders understand that commitment inevitably leads to success.
- Victorious leaders know how to build a unified team that's greater than the sum of its parts.

UNCOMPROMISING QUALITIES OF EFFECTIVE LEADERSHIP

1. Surround yourself with people smarter than you

2. Acknowledge mistakes when you make them. Take corrective actions, learn from them, and move on

3. Maximize the potential of your employees

4. Be selfless. Serve your employees and your organization. Make personal gain an afterthought. The desire for personal gain may color your judgment on what is best for the team as a whole.

QUALITIES OF A GOOD LEADER

1.   Self-confidence & Belief:

I feel this is the most important trait on this leadership qualities list because without it most of the other qualities on the list wouldn't be possible. If you don't yet believe in yourself, try to change the way you feel through the use of positive affirmations and incantations every day.

It is only when you have self-confidence that other people will begin to follow you. If you don't believe me, ask yourself if you would follow someone who was unsure of themselves?

2.   Self-Awareness & Self-Mastery:

This means that you must be able to control your mind, your thoughts, your feelings and desires at all times. This type of self-awareness and mastery are essential especially in times of conflict or confrontation. The best way to gain control when your mind or emotions start to take over is to breathe deeply.

This is #2 on the leadership qualities list because you will often have to deal with people or situations that would make someone who's not in control of their mind and feelings curl up and quit. Also, it's essential to master this to maintain your focus so that you can accomplish everything that must be done in a leadership position.

3.   Patience:

This quality will grow much stronger only after you've truly mastered yourself. When you can control your emotions and thoughts, you will be able to maintain patience even in the most stressful situations.

You often hear the phrase "patience is a virtue", and this is very true. Having patience will allow you to be more understanding of another's situation or position, which will ultimately allow you to better lead that person toward their goal.

4.   Understanding & Empathy:

Notice how this leadership qualities list ties together. Having patience will allow for better understanding and empathy towards a teammate's thoughts, feelings, situation, etc... Only when you truly understand someone can you truly help that person. The reason being is that there is no 'one' solution that is the fix-all.

5.   Attentiveness:

This leadership qualities list would not be complete without this important trait. When you're dealing with people, if you're un-attentive you'll never be able to have a true understanding of what your team needs to succeed. This is also going to play into the power of influence because you will not be able to influence a person without knowing what they really need.

6.   Integrity:

I almost can't put a rating on any one trait in this leadership qualities list, because they all are equally important. You can learn to lead people and become successful, but if you want to maintain your position for an extended period of time you'll have to gain your team's trust. You must do things for the overall good of the team and not just think about yourself or the here-and-now. Sure, you can make a quick buck in network marketing or any form of sales if you don't care about others, but it will never last.

7.   Decisiveness:

This is perhaps one of the easiest and most difficult qualities to master. The leadership qualities list wouldn't be complete without decisiveness. You must possess all ten of the other qualities in order to achieve this trait, or at least to effectively be decisive.

8.   Pay attention:

Pay attention to that last sentence, because you can be decisive and reckless at the same time. A leader can and will make decisions quickly based on intuition, and will usually stick with that decision long enough to know if it was a good decision or not. If you're someone who takes weeks to make a .50 cent decision, the opportunity will certainly pass you by.

9.   Takes Initiative:

Once you've made a decision in your mind, the next step would be to take action. A leader is willing to take initiative with a total uncertainty of success or failure. Again this doesn't mean that you should be reckless, but you must be willing to lose some battles in order to learn how to win the war. Taking initiative also means that you don't procrastinate in all areas of your life. Followers sit back and wait for the leader to tell them it's safe to take the action. What do you want to be?

10.   Responsibility:

Nearing the end of this leadership qualities list is responsibility. You alone are responsible for your success. When you understand this and can admit to yourself and others when you're not doing what is required, you'll be able to push harder and further to achieve greater success. With that being said, you're only partly responsible for the success of your team. You can show them the way, but if they choose not to follow your path, they are responsible for their failures.

11.   The power of Influence:

This power is not to be used immorally, which is why I've waited until now to add it to the leadership qualities list. Having a deep desire to truly help other people become successful will increase your power of influence greatly. People can sense if you're someone who wants to help them or not. Therefore, the power of influence can only be harnessed after you are able to understand people at their core and show them that you care about what happens to them. One way this can be achieved is by taking a genuine interest in their well being or professional growth.

When you have harnessed the power of influence by developing this leadership qualities list within you, you will not have to convince people to do anything or buy anything. They will simply take action because they desire to.

In closing, take note that it's important for you to begin with self-mastery so that you have the mindset and control to properly develop the rest of the qualities on this leadership qualities list.

It's also essential to develop these qualities in order to become a leader. Lastly, I want to mention that the power of influence will develop naturally as the other qualities become greater. Work through developing these qualities and characteristics in order, and you'll truly become a great leader.

No matter how good you currently are, no matter how intelligent you may be, no matter how many awards you have won, you will fail eventually if you are not a selfless leader.

Remember all the leadership qualities discussed above – Bookmark it, do something. You can be a great leader. Effective leadership is within your reach. It starts by understanding the leadership qualities and how to incorporate them into your day to day activities.

The good news is . . . these attributes can be learned. And . . . this is your big chance.

CHAPTER FOUR
HOW TO MANAGE PEOPLE

Over the years, we have seen dramatic changes and evolution in the types of skills that a manager should possess in order to be successful. The business world is more competitive and fast-paced than ever before, and a great manager can make a major difference in the amount of success experienced by any organization. The biggest change that managers have had to adapt to over the years is that it has become increasingly important that they understand how to manage people. A manager who knows how to develop a good relationship, inspire, and motivate other members of his or her organization will not only have a great advantage over many of their competitors, but will also have a much more promising future than those who fail to understand how to manage people.

Not long ago, a manager of a successful software company called together his team of software engineers to discuss the purchase and use of a new software program to help with certain types of analysis that needed to be performed. The manager had chosen a software program that he felt would meet the needs of the team after researching the different options available on his own. The software was very expensive, but it worked well and performed the analysis that the team of engineers needed. However, the manager noticed a great deal of resistance from his team members when it came to using the software.

Wisely, the manager called the team together to address their reluctance to use the new software program. He invited them to research the available programs and choose one that they felt was the best fit for the team. The team chose a program very similar to the one that had been originally chosen, and immediately they were happy to use the new software. The difference in the performance of the analysis tools was minimal, but the fact that the team who would be using the software was able to choose the best fitting option made a huge difference to the software engineers.

This manager learned an important lesson. Both software packages were able to perform the necessary analysis, but asking his team of software engineers which software package they would like to use caused the engineers to be fully engaged and excited about the new tools that were available to them. The manager was asking his team to make a change, but instead of seeking their input to make the change flow as smoothly as possible, he pushed his choice upon his team.

One of the key lessons to learn in managing people is that people don't resist change nearly as much as they resist being changed. Change in business is inevitable and it usually leads to growth and greater business results. However, if a manager asks team members to help find a solution rather than forcing a solution upon them, there is a much better chance that employees will "buy in" to the change. It's a subtle difference, but one that can make a tremendous difference and lead to much more positive results.

HOW TO BE AN EFFECTIVE MANAGER

The title of Manager carries with it much prestige and usually a pay raise. This is probably one of the most sought after titles in organizations. Many workers strive to become managers and seek the status and the perks along with it.

However, once the coveted title is acquired the reality is very different from the fantasy. New managers find very quickly that the job is not at all what they thought. Managing people can be extremely challenging. Even with multiple business degrees, there aren't many programs that teach how to be an effective manager. This chapter helps to map out some of the qualities you need in order to be an effective manager.

1.   Effective managers need to like people

The first quality of a good manager is that you need to genuinely like people. Effective managers like and respect people. Understand that in order to get anything done, you need people working together to accomplish a common goal. You should want to see your employees excel. Also, it helps your effectiveness if you actually care about your employees. Liking and caring about your employees is not something that can be faked.

The programs a manager suggests or puts into place demonstrates whether they truly care about their staff. I once worked for a company that didn't want to offer a CPR class to the employees because they were more concerned about being sued. The employees wanted the class because of the strenuous working conditions, but when the managers refused to allow the class, the employees felt the managers didn't truly care about their well-being.

2.   Effective managers need to be good communicators

Communication is vitally important to relate with your employees. Allow your employees to communicate with you any news regarding the projects they are working on, the company, or customer problems. Encourage your team to submit suggestions for process improvements. Likewise, you need to have open communication process with your workers regarding company changes, especially changes that affect them directly. If you don't communicate openly and honestly with your employees they will feel blind sighted by the lack of communication and resent you for it.

3.   Effective managers know how to build morale

There are many managers that feel building morale is not their responsibilities. However, when the morale of your employees is down, the production of your company is also down. No one argues that the responsibility of the manager is to keep up production. Therefore, if it is the responsibility of the manager to keep up production and production is down because of low morale, then it is the responsibility of the manager to increase morale.

4.   Effective managers train employees

According to Bill Gates, Founder of Microsoft, a good manager trains their employees to do the job better than they can. We know that training is important to enhance the skills of employees. However, most managers keep certain skills for themselves because they're afraid of losing their jobs if their employees can do it better than they can. If this is true for you, talk to your boss and discuss what additional opportunities are open for you. You and your employees should be increasing and growing in your skill sets.

5.   Effective managers recognize and reward employees

Rewarding your employees will go a long way toward encouraging and motivating them. However, not all rewards are created equal. Every successful reward should be created specifically to the person who receives it.

This means that offering money as a reward for a job well done will not motivate all of your employees in the same way. Bob Nelson, author of 1001 Ways to Reward Employees, suggests that managers should give rewards that show true appreciation. The motivation generated will be far greater than a token gift that has little significance.

6.   Effective managers are always learning

A truly effective manager is always learning how to be a better manager. Never think that you know everything there is to know about managing people. You may not be aware of it, but there are four generations in the workforce today. There is plenty to be learned about how to get all of these people to work together. New books, on the subject of management, are released monthly. Reading informational material regularly and even taking a course every now and then will keep your skills as a manager current. Everyone in your company will benefit from your continued pursuit of excellence.

CHAPTER FIVE

MANAGEMENT STYLES

WHAT IS MANAGEMENT STYLE?

'What is management style' can be answered in a few different ways. Traditionally, we have focused on how the manager relates to subordinates when we consider this issue. Leadership style is just another way of talking about the same subject. The question of style is meant to address the issue of how best to motivate employees to do what the manager wants them to do. Clearly, the most effective management style is the one that gets the most productivity out of all employees.

Here is a new slant on how effective managers behave. Some managers have a very proactive style. They plan ahead. Others are typically reactive. They don't care if they don't anticipate problems, and are happy to improvise. Managers can also be supportive or punitive in how they treat employees. The best managers are proactive and supportive. Reactive managers don't really manage at all. They just... react.

1.   The Reactive Management Style

This style is very common. Such managers are often punitive as well. Reactive managers don't really enjoy the management process. They got promoted by being functional experts. In management, they still want to do what they most enjoy doing - devise expert solutions. They may hold regular meetings on a proactive basis, but they want competent subordinates who can get on with their work without bothering them. However, they want subordinates to come to them if they have a problem.

2.   The Punitive Reactive Manager

No one likes to hear about problems. Reactive managers with a punitive style don't intend to be mean. They just get annoyed when they hear that a project might be off the rails. They may not always lose their temper, but their irritation is still visible in their tone of voice and body language. Their immediate priority is to fix the problem. They convey the message that they hope their subordinates have learned from their mistakes and won't let it happen again.

This is punitive: It instills a fear of failure in team members and makes them hesitate to inform managers about problems in the future. A punitive style increases the likelihood of further errors and an early departure from the company.

3.   The Reactive Supportive Manager

Reactive supportive managers also want subordinates to operate independently. However, when problems are brought to them, they behave like a coach, a sounding board, and a helper or enabler. They help subordinates see what went well, commend them for good efforts and help them learn from their mistakes in an encouraging manner. But, this is still not the most effective management style. Management is an investment. To manage resources invested, it is imperative to prevent errors before they happen. This means being proactive.

4.   The Proactive Punitive Manager

Such managers meet with staff frequently. They have such a fear of failure that their anxiety to avoid error is punitively communicated to their teams. They are always asking questions about progress in a tone that creates fear in their teams and motivates them to hide mistakes if possible. AKA – The micro manager.

5.   The Proactive Supportive Manager

These managers also hold regular meetings, but staff are asked to talk about what has gone well since the last meeting before the discussion moves on to problems. Issues are anticipated and avoided by cultivating an atmosphere of safety and openness. Positive feedback that is genuinely felt is offered and employees are encouraged to think of solutions to problems in a supportive, coaching manner.

Naturally, proactive supportive managers deal firmly with serious performance problems but they are more effective than the other styles because they cultivate a positive team spirit.

DIFFERENT MANAGEMENT STYLES

There are many different management styles that can be adopted by different people in a position of leadership. Often times, chosen leadership skills will depend heavily on personality types, but it's also worth thinking about the desired outcome of your management.

1.   Autocratic leadership

The Autocratic management style is based on decision making. The leader in this situation will make decisions quickly and effectively, with little room for argument but also little room for error. The benefits of this management style are the results; if you trust yourself to get things done right, then you don't spend much time awake at night worrying about how your business is being run.

But, as the name suggests, this management style is authoritarian and can make employees resentful if mishandled. With little room for argument comes little room for your employees to grow in certain skills sets, which is something they may be concerned about.

2.   Democratic leadership

Democratic leadership is pretty much what it sounds like. By involving employees in some of the inner workings of the management mind, this style encourages open communication and joint decision-making. To a certain extent, your staff will have a free reign to display their skills and learn more about your approach.

On the other hand, this style of working is more chaotic than autocratic leadership. You'll have a lot of opinions on one topic and it can cause argument and a slower decision-making process in general. But with the risk, this management style comes with the possibility of a more dynamic and diverse workforce that feels supported and enthused to tackle any issues that may arise.

3.   Catalytic leadership

With a Catalytic management style, leaders make all the decisions, but consciously in the best interests of their employees.

Catalytic management encourages an open relationship between employer and employee, in which there is a safe place to share thoughts and feelings and a feeling of support in the event of something going wrong.

However, the basis of the catalytic management style is still very much authoritative - the leader assumes the responsibility for all decisions and, by running each of these decisions past staff and ensuring them of their safety and wellbeing, it can slow the process down considerably.

FINDING YOUR MANAGEMENT STYLE

Each individual is naturally suited to a certain type of management style, but it all comes down to the results you want to achieve. Do you want your workforce to be dynamic, proactive and enthusiastic? Do you want to minimize the risk of mistakes and disagreement?

It's important to remember that, like everything else, leadership skills are not always easily defined. Each of the management styles listed above are unique and none are written in stone. It's all about what is appropriate for your business and your working relationships, which may well be a mix of the three. I like to call these hybrids.

DEVELOP YOUR OWN MANAGEMENT STYLE

Each individual in any management position has developed a management style, a behavioral approach to managing others. In this section, I will address the 3 styles.

1. The Autocratic style

2. The Democratic style

3. The Catalytic style.

Let's define each and the most outstanding single characteristics of each style.

1. The Autocratic Style (natural style): Dictator; My way or the highway approach; I'm in Charge here and you are to do as I said; don't think, just act and do it NOW; Demands respect from everyone even if it has not yet been earned; Call me Mr. or Mrs. or Sir/Madam.

2. The Democratic Style (natural style): Close friend; Father figure; No one ever makes a mistake; Any and all results are acceptable; Take your time we'll get it done when we can; Acccepts any and all suggestions from subordinates even if the suggestion may be wrong' Does not discipline or control the staff; Staff controls the manager; Has a great need to be liked by everyone at every level; Call me by my first name.

3. The Catalytic Style (Learned/developed blended style): Teacher style; Trainer; Developer of subordinates; Coaching style; Teach what they know and show as they go style; Strives to achieve results above expectations; Explains plans; Details expectations; Maintains control but expects input from all

subordinates; Is respected by subordinates and by all management because respect has been earned through performance.

At first glance, it might appear the style that is the best of the 3 styles is the Catalytic.

Each style has its appropriate time and place and each can be successful under specific circumstances. Management styles are developed by the individual and are natural tendencies. We are all influenced throughout our business career by those around us who have managed us as we ascend into management positions ourselves. Our developed style can begin as early as grade school and further develop in high school and college. When we enter the workforce and begin to report to our first supervisor/manager, our future management style begins to evolve even further.

When the time comes and we are promoted into our first management position, many want to be like their first manager. This could be a positive evolution or perhaps a negative one.

Let's assume, for this exercise, that our first manager was a really wonderful person, very friendly with the entire staff, and displayed a father figure management style. People who report to this manager, including you, may not have performed as well as you could have because your boss was such a nice person. Almost any type of performance was considered acceptable, including less than expected results.

This management style, although comfortable to all of the direct reporters, may not be as effective as it could be and the results achieved may be found to be unacceptable to upper management.

You may recognize that this is an example of a Democratic management style and although well-liked by all, you may not have an extended shelf life as a manager due to the lack of acceptable performance.

Let's address another example of management style, the Autocratic. This manager has very high, almost unreasonable expectations which you are to live up to at all times. If you don't, it becomes a watch-out environment. This manager usually raises his or her voice when speaking to any person on their staff, pounds their fist on the table at meetings, criticizes in public and rarely shares any praise to any member of the staff. This style usually doesn't explain plans of action or details of expectations. This manager deictates duties and responsibilities, usually does not welcome input from the workers, rejects suggestions and usees verbal force at every turn. Remember, under certain circumstances and conditions this may be the management style needed.

Example: Upper management has a department filled with very qualified, experienced and talented employees who, under their present democratic manager are performing below acceptable results. Now it is time for a change. Consider someone who has a natural autocratic management style. Why? A drastic change in results is necessary and critical to the overall performance within the organization. A person who is going to go into this department with the sole mission of cracking the whip to get the job done and quickly turn results around is who you want. The downside danger, however, is employee fallout. Some may look at it as cleaning house or weeding out the weak employees, while others disagree whole heartedly with the style of management in any scenario.

There may be some fallout because of the sudden change in management style, but the best of the staff will typically rise to the demands of the new manager, especially in this job market... Especially if their goal is to stay with the organization and to move forward with their careers.

We can readily recognize a severe change in the sports world. A football team has had the same coach for several years and in the last year or so the team has not had a winning record, has not qualified for any playoff games and ownership is now faced with a coaching change. You have witnessed a change from a long-term democratic coach to a dictator autocratic style head coach and staff. The very next season the team is now a winning organization and goes to the playoffs. Keep in mind an autocratic style manager/coach usually has a short shelf life, perhaps 2-3 seasons and then another change will have to be made. This is typically where ownership starts looking for the blended management style coach, the Catalytic coach.

The Catalytic manager/coach, due to the fact that this is a blended style of both the Autocratic and the Democratic styles will now have a long shelf live with the department/team and will more than likely produce winning results on a consistent basis. Now, obviously this isn't an exact science, but time and time again have proven that there is a consistency to this madness.

Can an autocratic and democratic management style change to become a catalytic manager?

Yes. The catalytic is not a natural style like the other two styles. The catalytic style is learned and developed over a period of time. What is needed to develop the catalytic style is proper training and direction from a strong catalytic manager who is willing to take the other style individuals under their wing and spend time changing their approach to managing subordinates. This typically includes training and developing to cause a change in their behavioral tendencies and their approach to others.

CHOOSING YOUR MANAGEMENT STYLE

Management styles are the different practices and traits that are utilized everyday in making decisions and relating to subordinates while conducting business. Managers have to perform many roles in an organization and exactly how they handle these many complex situations will be the tell-tale sign of their style of management.

Management and leadership styles work together with the skills that are learned to influence their staff and to promote increased motivation and performance. However, it is not just a matter of choosing an individual style. Managers will generally gravitate towards the style that best fits their personalities and characteristics. These management styles tend to change the culture and the skills of the employees in any set work environment. The key to becoming a successful manager is the ability of the manager to adapt to the changing face of the workplace while remaining diverse enough to keep their practices consistent. A major problem in numerous work environments is that the management styles change too frequently and do not remain consistent. The same can also be said for management styles stuck in the stone age and haven't changed or adapted in decades.

Focusing on the rapid changes in the information technology field and the growing number of multi-cultural work environments that outsourcing has created, consistent and stable management styles prove to be an asset. With the fast pace that technologies change, so does the need to keep employees up to date and on top of the best technology available. During this process, more and more companies opt for younger and more recent educated employees, thus less seasoned and experienced. With the absence of the experience, the newer and younger managers tend to emulate management styles from their past or present management teams as their own. This can prove to be a very weak link in the successful operation of the business due to the adapted style, maybe one that is not cohesive with their new manager's personality or experience.

A few of the most common traits of good management and employee working environment are:

1.   Team Work:

Creating an environment where everyone is working together and striving for the same common goal instead of the "I'm the boss and you do what I say" type of working relationship.

2.   Consistency:

Keep the working relationship consistent and avoid confusing the "Office Personality" and "Home Personality". This will set its own limits within the working relationship.

3.   Ownership:

Make sure the whole team remains engaged in every facet of the job or project and help them to take ownership on their part.

4.   Communication:

Maintain communication at all times and keep yourself available. Avoid offering an "Open Door Policy" if it will be used to evaluate one's work. Communication between management and employees can make all the difference in the world.

5.   Inclusion:

Keep in mind that the production and the consistency of the employees is a key factor in evaluating and displaying the effectiveness of the management. Make sure that each and every employee has a sense of value to the team and the end result.

Although these are minor points, each and every one can be continually expanded as to their relevancy to any industry. But in a bigger picture, the managers of today can learn an enormous amount from the managers of yesterday. The laws and practices are constantly changing and a successful manager cannot sit back and wait for a new class. Be proactive and find all of the information you can on the management style that best fits you and your work environment, and put it to use.

CHAPTER SIX

DEALING WITH CONFLICTS IN THE WORKPLACE

Conflict is a major concern in both your personal and working life. If not dealt with quickly, tactfully, and efficiently, conflict can lead to serious confrontation and/or a complete breakdown of relationships. It can even lead to violent or even dangerous situations.

A conflict can stem from a minor complaint that was not resolved and left to fester. This can then gradually grow into an insurmountable problem. A conflict can be as innocent as a sibling rivalry - arguing over a toy - to a dispute with a customer or colleague over a product, service or procedure, to a war between countries in extreme cases.

There will be times during the course of your professional career where you will have to deal with complaints and conflicts. Your successful handling of these situations will have a direct bearing on you and your organization's reputation for customer service and its continued success.

WHAT CAUSES CONFLICT?

Conflicts normally occur when people have different ideas and believe they have the superior viewpoint. This is particularly true of conflict in the workplace - among colleagues and/or management. The issue becomes one of power, of gaining control or of 'being proved right'. To resolve this type of conflict it is necessary to move from the power clash to one of service and responsibility - to work for the good of the group rather than the individuals within it. In resolving a conflict it should be more important to make sure that both parties' needs are met rather than winning the argument.

Conflict can also be caused by a lack of communication or by a failure to recognize the needs of another person. Whatever the scenario, the main component in conflict is a misunderstanding. These misunderstandings can occur due to differences in age, culture, race or religion.

Conflict situations can include customer related issues, misunderstandings or communication barriers, as well as conflict among colleagues.

1. Conflicts due to customer-related issues.

A complaint, no matter how trivial it might sound to you, is legitimate in the eyes of the customer and must be taken seriously. Customers come into your organization to do business. They have a need and they believe (or hope) that you will be able to fulfill that need. They are willing to pay you for your time, effort and service and they expect your full and undivided attention. If they do not receive this attention or a satisfactory product or service, then they are not receiving value for their money and then have every right to complain.

2. Conflicts arising out of customer related issues may include:

a. Problems or faults with services or products. The customer has not received the quality of service or product that they expected and are unhappy enough about it to complain. A complaint of this nature can be fairly easily resolved if the parties involved are prepared to communicate and compromise.

b. Delays or poor timing of a product or service supplied. The customer has been kept waiting longer than expected or advised for their product or service and, as in the point above, become upset at the delay. Delays can cause a great deal of inconvenience for customers, particularly if they have made time to be on hand and are then disappointed.

c. Difficult or demanding customers. Some customers are hard to please and are, by nature, very demanding and aggressive. If they are not handled carefully they could, potentially, become threatening.

d. Drug or alcohol related issues. These could include being refused entry or ejection from premises due to their condition and the risk they represent to other customers or staff.

3. Conflicts due to misunderstandings or communication barriers.

No two people are exactly alike - not even twins. People have different points of view brought about by the many influences in their lives.

These influences include:

a. Genetics: The genes that we inherit from our parents and over which we have no control. These might involve the color of our eyes and hair, to our health.

b. Upbringing: Which involves the way in which our parents raised us and the values they instilled in us.

c. Culture and religion: This influences the things that we believe to be true and the customs and traditions we follow.

d. Economics: Our view on life can be strongly influenced by our economic situation, whether we are financially comfortable or struggling to make ends meet.

e. Education: Our level of education will also have a large impact on what we think and how we view the world.

f. The environment: This means the environment in which we operate: Our neighborhoods, housing situations, and the people we are surrounded by.

g. Life experience: This nvolves all the experiences we have had in our lives, the successes, and failures, the lessons we have learned from these experiences and the many roles that we have played to date.

All of these things and more go into making us the individuals we are. Our thoughts and feelings about almost everything we come into contact with will be shaped by these influences. So, we have our own opinions and points of view on a whole range of ideas and areas, and these sometimes clash with other peoples' viewpoints. These clashes can take the form of a lively but friendly debate, while they can just as easily become heated and aggravated and degenerate into shouting matches - The beginnings of a conflict.

We can avoid these situations by reaching an understanding between the parties. This can be done by communicating openly and honestly, being willing to listen to the other person's point of view - remembering that the influences that have shaped their beliefs and viewpoints could be very different to yours - but no less valid.

Misunderstandings and communication barriers can occur because:

A. People do not listen to each other with an eye to reaching an understanding

B. People are not prepared to compromise in order to resolve the situation

C. People do not understand cultural differences and are not prepared to make allowances for them.

To resolve a conflict situation, steps need to be taken to bring the two points of view closer - to reach a compromise that both parties can accept. Part of strong conflict resolution skills is the art of communication and recognizing the barriers to a good two-way communications flow.

These barriers can include:

I.   Not paying attention

Customers or colleagues who are trying to communicate with you will feel ignored and frustrated if you allow yourself to become distracted. Not paying attention to them is rude and unprofessional and stops the communication flow. The result of this could be the loss of a customer, a complaint about you to your manager, or a loss of respect. Do not allow yourself to be distracted - focus your attention on what is being said and really listen to your customer or colleague. If you must interrupt the conversation to answer the phone, or speak with another staff member, excuse yourself politely.

II.   Not looking at a person

Maintaining reasonable eye contact with the person you are communicating with is very important. It shows you are paying attention and that you are interested. By not looking at the person who is talking to you, you are indicating not only disinterest but are also making them feel uncomfortable. They may think you are not being honest or trustworthy - you may be trying to hide something from them.

III.   Interrupting

Interrupting someone when they are talking is a major barrier to open and can easily cause conflict. Once again, you are indicating that you are not interested in what they have to say. Breaking into what they are saying to make your own thoughts known, or worse, to finish their sentences for them is no way to gain a proper understanding of another person's needs and expectations. Allow them to finish what they are saying and pay attention. If, for some reason, the conversation needs to be wound up, then take control by asking leading or closing questions that allow for short answers only.

IV.   Tone of voice

The tone of voice used during a conversation can also start a conflict. Arrogance, demand, anger, whining, disinterest, etc. can all add a tone to the voice that can cause people to react negatively. When dealing with customers or colleagues, you should keep your tone friendly, calm, and pleasant. At the very least, if you do feel annoyed, you should try and keep the tone of your voice neutral.

V.   Sarcasm

Sarcasm has no place in any conversation between two people and is an open invitation for conflict (Yes, there are appropriate times in social settings, but hardly ever in a professionl business setting). There are times, in everyone's working life, when you think "If I get asked one more stupid question, I'll go mad!", but sarcasm in the face of a silly question or remark does nothing but hurt the other person and, possibly, dent their self-esteem. We often forget that not everyone knows everything we do about our industry - in fact most customers know very little about the tourism and hospitality industries. The same goes for clients in a bank or patients in a doctor's office. We can forgive our customers or junior colleagues, therefore, for asking questions that may have obvious answer. Show patience and understanding - it's just as easy as and much more pleasant than giving a sarcastic or snide answer.

VI.   Rudeness

There is never any excuse for rudeness. A respectful and courteous attitude on your part should avoid or defuse any antagonism a person brings with them into your office. Should you find yourself nevertheless, dealing with a person with whom you simply cannot get along with - rudeness is not the solution. Speak to your supervisor or manager and ask for their advice.

VII.   Cultural differences

Cultural differences can be the source of a great many conflicts. When dealing with people from other countries, other beliefs and so on, it is easy to misunderstand words, gestures, and customs. If you want to excel at your profession, it is a good idea to familiarize yourself with some of the more prevalent customs of other cultures. On the whole, however, people from all over the world, from all walks of life and from all creeds respond well to respectful and courteous behavior. Do not make fun of customs you don't understand. Treat everyone you deal with, both customers and colleagues, with respect and you should do very well.

Any one of these points could provoke a customer or a colleague into complaining - which could then, potentially, turn into a conflict. It is a good idea, therefore, to remain courteous and polite when dealing with other people.

SIGNS OF A POTENTIAL CONFLICT

A conflict does not happen suddenly. People do not go from calm and cool one moment to angry and aggressive the next. Well, sometimes, but usually this has something to do with an underlying problem which has been festering for a while.

For the most part, conflict builds. It may take hours, weeks or even years. However long the process takes, there are always signs that a conflict is building. If these signs are recognized early, steps can be taken to quickly and efficiently resolve the situation before it becomes a major issue.

Early signs of conflict can include (but are not limited to):

- Aggressive body language: Narrowed eyes or flared nostrils - a sure sign of building anger as the person takes a deep breath, either to control themselves or to go on the attack; Stretched

muscles in the face and jaw line - tightened in building anger and aggression; Tapping fingers or feet - shows impatience
- Malicious or negative gossip among colleagues
- Difficulty in discussing an issue calmly and rationally
- Tone of voice - indicating boredom, sarcasm, irritation

These are all signs of irritation, dissatisfaction or impatience. If you recognize any of these signs when dealing with a complaint or a conflict, you should RUN AWAY! Just joking... endeavor to find out the reasons why the other person is starting to feel impatient or irritated. You can do this by asking relevant questions and listening carefully to their answers. In this way, you can reach an understanding of the issue at hand and perhaps avoid escalating the situation.

If not recognized and acted upon these signs can then be followed by:

a. Raised voice - speaking rapidly in a loud, high-pitched voice - or even shouting

b. Body leaning forward in an effort to intimidate

c. Hand gestures - finger poking and pointing in an aggressive manner.

d. Refusal to cooperate

e. Storming out of a room, slamming doors, drawers or implements

At this point, you may already have a conflict and it will take careful handling to bring the situation back under control.

CRISIS SITUATIONS

Complaints can escalate into conflict and conflict, and if not resolved effectively, can potentially escalate into a crisis. People wish to be taken seriously. If they are not, or are repeatedly ignored, they can become aggressive and a threat to safety and security of the organization and the people in it. Equally, people who are under the influence of drugs or alcohol, and are not in control of themselves, can present a danger to those around them if they are not handled carefully.

Situations where personal safety of customers or colleagues may be threatened and assistance required may involve:

- Drug or alcohol affected persons
- People with guns or other weapons
- Situations where someone has been or may be hurt
- People who appear to be violent or threatening
- Situations where customers refuse to leave or to be pacified.

In these cases, it is extremely important to:

- Calm yourself and to try and calm the other person.
- Move them, discreetly, out of the main area of your office or shop
- Take note of details of the problem for future reference

- Do not argue with a person who is visibly upset or aggressive as this will only compound the situation.
- Bring in the assistance of relevant management, security and/or authorities such as police as soon as possible.

ORGANIZATIONAL REQUIREMENTS

You cannot simply make a conflict go away by giving the complaining party whatever they want. Resolving a conflict is a delicate balance between reaching an agreement between parties while at the same time staying within the constraints of your organization's requirements and policies.

These constraints may include:

1.   Costs Issues:

Often times, a conflict with a customer will be centered on dissatisfaction with a product or service. If the product or service was actually found to be faulty, then the simplest solution to the problem is a straightforward replacement. Sometimes, however, the situation is not as simple and the customer will demand further compensation. In these cases, a replacement may not be enough and something extra may need to be done. When determining the extent of compensation, if any, to be offered to the client, there are a few issues to consider.

These may include:

- Customer good will & repeat business. If your organization is dependent on customers coming back again, this is an important consideration.
- Organization reputation. A dissatisfied customer can tell many people that they received bad service from an organization who did not meet their needs and this can lead to a loss of business. This is especially true with the use of social media or review sites such as Yelp.
- Direct cost. Compensation to a client can be in the form of cash, additional products or services, or an upgrade to the product or service they have purchased. If compensation is to be of a monetary nature, then the cost to the organization must be considered.

RESOLVING CONFLICT SITUATIONS

When a person has purchased a product or service from your organization and it is not what they expected it to be, or does not perform properly they will feel dissatisfied and disappointed. As a consequence, when this person complains they generally believe that they have a legitimate reason for doing so and they may do so long and heatedly to the first person they come in contact with. This might be you - even though you had nothing to do with the original sale and have never met the customer. The worst thing you can do is tell them it's not your problem.

Take ownership of the issue, regardless of whether you were involved in the problem or not. "Passing the buck" at this point is not going to help matters. The customer approached you, so deal with the issue and don't pass them off saying "It's not my problem" or "The lady who handled this is not here now...." At that particular moment in time the customer does not see you, the individual, they see you, the representative of the company. So it is you, the representative of the company, they expect to help them.

If you were not part of the original transaction where the problem occurred, get as much information as you can from the customer to help determine what to do. For example, you can ask:

- Exactly what the problem is
- When and where it occurred
- How long ago the problem occurred?
- What did they pay for the product or service?

How they see the situation is resolved - this will give you an idea of the person's expectations and how they impact on the organization's policies and procedures.

If the person who was involved in the original transaction is available, you should ask them to join the discussion in order to get both sides of the picture.

It is very important, however, to keep to the issue at hand and not to let emotions or ego get in the way of finding a solution to the problem. Stay calm, listen to all points of view with an open mind and try to keep the communication process flowing in a positive manner.

Finding a solution to a conflict involves a certain set of skills and techniques. It takes a step by step approach to ensure a positive outcome for all parties concerned.

STEPS IN RESOLVING CONFLICT

Finding a solution to a conflict will often become a matter of "give and take" where one party makes a suggestion that may not be entirely acceptable to the other. When this happens you will need to define the issues as seen by all parties and negotiate a mutually acceptable outcome. This will normally happen in a logical sequence:

- Define the problem
- Work out what you want out of the conflict
- Brainstorm for options
- Evaluate solutions
- Decide on solutions

1.   Define the problem

Everyone involved in the conflict needs to agree on a definition of the problem before it can be solved. This could mean describing the problem in terms of each person's needs and understanding of the issue at hand. Questions to consider might include:

- What is the problem? Is it only my problem? Who else is involved?
- Can I solve it? Can it be solved in general?
- Is this the real problem or merely a symptom of a larger one?
- Does it need an immediate solution or can it wait? Is it likely to go away by itself? Can I risk ignoring it?
- Does the problem have ethical dimensions?
- What conditions must the solution satisfy?

- Will the solution affect something that must remain unchanged?
- Will I need help?

Asking these types of questions will outline what all the issues are from various perspectives giving you a firm foundation for exploring options. Depending on the nature of the problem and what it will take to resolve it, it might in extreme cases even be worth letting the matter go. It is important to keep a customer satisfied, but not at all costs. If a customer is being completely unreasonable and demanding, then sometimes it is the better option to lose that customer. Not every time, but in some cases this may happen.

2.   Work out what you want out of the conflict

You also need to develop a clear understanding of the expected outcome. This could be: An agreement on acceptable compensation for faulty products or services; A better relationship with the other party; A mutually acceptable solution to an ongoing work issue; For the other person to respect your opinion. With firm expectations of what would be an acceptable outcome in mind, you can then begin to negotiate with the other party until an agreement has been reached.

3.   Brainstorm for options

When all parties concerned have had the opportunity to explain their feelings on the matter, then all of the issues should be out in the open. At this point, you can look at the various options available. There might be a number of solutions to the problem which could work for everyone involved. Don't get stuck on one solution just because it's the first one you find. Be creative about

115

the possibilities available to you, and look for common ground. You can decide from the options later.

4.   Evaluate solutions

In deciding the best result from the options available, you should weigh up the pros and cons of each one based on the organization's policies and procedures, cost or budgetary constraints, legal ramifications and mutual benefit. When discussing and evaluating options it is often the case that each party will prefer an option that most closely gives them what they want regardless of its impact on the other party. In these cases, you need to negotiate and compromise so that an agreement that both parties are satisfied with can be reached.

THE ART OF COMPROMISE

Compromise does not mean giving in or losing. It means looking for ways to meet each other's needs by making concessions to the other party involved. Compromise involves negotiating what you are, or are not, prepared to do in order to get what you want.

You should be open to good arguments rather than pressure or manipulation from the other party. Be open to reason but closed to threats. In difficult conflicts, it might be necessary to bring in another person to mediate. This person might need to be skilled, mutually respected, and not have a personal interest in the outcome.

Decide on a mutually acceptable solution - When all available options have been tabled and considered, then you can decide on the best one - the one that keeps both parties happy! Make sure each person takes responsibility for agreeing with the decision. This may take the form of a written agreement or contract, or a letter outlining what was agreed to.

Separate your feelings from the problem. When your emotions get tangled up in the pros and cons of an argument, you can't always reach the best conclusion. If you take a strong position because of the way you feel, you can't work out the best solution to the problem because your perception of it is controlled by emotions which are likely to have nothing to do with the problem. It's not about who is right or wrong. Arguing over whose fault it is or placing blame will do nothing but increase tension and get in the way of resolving the situation. You should not let your feelings get in the way. Points that can help here include:

a. Act and speak calmly. Arguing with a customer or colleague could result in a full-blown confrontation. Pause before making a response to them. This will give you time to collect yourself, to calm any irritation you might feel and also gives you a chance to work out how to phrase your response in the most appropriate way.

b. Try to put yourself in the other person's shoes; empathize with them. Use expressions such as "I can understand why you would feel that way" and encourage them to share their point of view.

c. Listen carefully and completely to what they are saying. Hear them out without interrupting them. Show you are interested through a positive listening attitude and ask clarifying questions to make sure you have understood them correctly.

d. Be patient and understanding. Don't interrupt them. Once they have had their say, they will generally be a lot calmer and easier to reason with. The problem can then often be resolved in a civilized manner.

e. At the appropriate time, acknowledge their point of view and ask them to give you the courtesy of now listening to your (organization's) position. For example; "I understand what you are saying, may I now explain our position to you, and then we can see how we can solve the problem together?"

DOCUMENTATION

Recording accurate information about complaints, conflicts and their outcomes is a very important part of any business. This type of information will show (among other things):

- Areas of the business that are not working properly
- Processes and procedures that need to be changed
- Things that customers like/or don't like about your products or services
- Gaps in the supply and demand of your products or services

With this information in hand, an organization can then use it to continually improve its products, services, image, and reputation.

Information can be recorded by way of (but not limited to):

Letters (or emails) of complaint. These should always be taken seriously. A written complaint should be answered immediately - even if it is simply to advise the customer of what will happen next. An investigation of the complaint should follow and the customer should then be advised of the outcome. A report of the complaint and the outcome should then be sent to the relevant supervisor or manager for any further action needed.

Notes taken during a phone call or after a face to face meeting. Once again, it is a good business practice to record the details of complaints or discussions about conflicts. These notes can be used for the organization's continuous improvement program, but they can also be used as reminders of the conversation should a dispute arise.

Formal documentation. These can be: Refund forms, Credit notes, Contracts, or agreement forms.

Evaluating conflict situations

It is a good business practice to continually look for ways in which an organization can improve its practices and procedures. One of the main ways an organization can do this is by seeking feedback - comments from customers, staff and other visitors to the organization. Reasons for seeking feedback may include:

- To ensure customer satisfaction and repeat business
- To maintain a reputation
- To learn from errors or mistakes
- To make improvements to the service/product delivery quality or to improve productivity and efficiency
- Follow up to see if the customer is satisfied in the case of a complaint or conflict

In a matter as important as a complaint or a conflict, feedback can also be sought by way of a phone call, letter or perhaps even a personal visit to the person concerned to ensure that any issue that existed between the conflicting parties has been successfully resolved.

When looking for how effective the solution to a conflict was, some of the questions that should be asked may include:

Why did this situation happen in the first place? A close examination of the circumstances surrounding the matter of conflict from both the customers and the organizations perspective can show problems in procedure, policy or product or service delivery. Issues to look at may include:

- Was there a breakdown in communication?
- Is the service delivery as good as it can be?
- Are the organization's policies and procedures as effective as they can be?
- Was the service/product faulty in some way?
- Did we resolve it effectively? This is a very important question from the customers and the organization's point of view.
- For the customer, resolving the problem effectively can mean that they are satisfied, that they have received value for their money and most importantly that they will probably continue to do business with you.
- For the organization, resolving the problem effectively can mean that they have retained a customer and kept within organizational guidelines and budgets

When looking at how the problem was resolved:

Ask critical questions about the outcome - was it the best possible option for everyone concerned? Did it cost your organization money? Too much money? Was the outcome worth the cost?

Evaluate the customer's reaction to your proposal - were they happy with it? Were they prepared to be reasonable? Will they continue to do business with you?

Compare the situation to any previous incidents of this nature. How was it handled last time? Is there a pattern emerging that should be addressed?

What can we do to prevent it from happening in the future? By looking at how the problem occurred in the first place and how effectively you resolved it, you can then take any necessary steps to prevent the same thing from happening again. This might mean: A change in policy or procedure; A change in a product or service; Training staff in customer service skills; Training staff in conflict and complaint handling.

By asking these, and other relevant questions, you can make improvements to the organization. This can lead to greater customer and staff satisfaction which will have a positive impact on the organization's continued success and prosperity.

CONCLUSION

Managing employee performance every day is the key to an effective performance management system. Setting goals, making sure your expectations are clear, and providing frequent feedback help people perform most effectively. The key components of a performance management system are:

1. Visibility

2. Clear expectations and accountability

3. Communication

4. Goals and rewards

A 2007 study by Towers Perrin found that 38 percent of workers are either partially or fully "disengaged." These are employees that are "just putting in time". Just 21 percent of employees reported being fully "engaged" enough to give their all for the team. The remaining 31 percent are considered "enrolled", otherwise good employees who lack an emotional connection to the company. Fully engaged employees are on average, 20% more productive and have a much higher retention rate. A comprehensive performance management program that incorporates the above tools will improve your employee engagement, which statistically has shown to increase productivity and lower costs.

Printed in Great Britain
by Amazon